NTC's
Dictionary
of
DEBATE

NTC's
Dictionary
of
DEBATE

Jim Hanson

National Textbook Company
a division of NTC *Publishing Group* • Lincolnwood, Illinois USA

1994 Printing

Published by National Textbook Company, a division of NTC Publishing Group.
© 1990 by NTC Publishing Group, 4255 West Touhy Avenue,
Lincolnwood (Chicago), Illinois 60646-1975 U.S.A.
Manufactured in the United States of America.
Library of Congress Catalog Card Number: 89-60183

4 5 6 7 8 9 VP 9 8 7 6 5 4 3

TO THE USER

The world of academic debate is an exciting environment involving thousands of people. It has its own practices, concepts, and even language. Debaters, coaches, and judges will often hear phrases like:

"Flip the disadvantage."

"The turn is taken out by the B point on criteria."

"This case has no inherency."

For the experienced debater or coach, these comments have meaning. For the beginner, this jargon is a barrier to joining the excitement. It is like listening to someone speak in an unfamiliar language—it just doesn't make sense.

So what does an inexperienced coach or debater do to make sense of debate jargon? Up until now, this question was difficult to answer. A debater who heard someone discuss the "uniqueness of a disadvantage" had few options. Very few textbooks include glossaries of debate terms. The few that do usually include definitions that are hard to understand. *Uniqueness* might be defined as "whether the element of the advantage or disadvantage will occur without the adoption of the proposition." This definition is fine for those who already know what *uniqueness* means, but it doesn't offer much help for the beginner.

For the advanced debater, judge, or coach, the lack of consistency among definitions also creates problems. What exactly is *inherency*? What is a *permutation*? What is a *value objection*? There is no textbook that defines all of these terms. In addition, there is no textbook that describes exactly how debate terms are used. What good is it if a debater learns the basic idea behind *criteria* only to make the nonsensical statement "We criteria our case"?

In *Advanced Debate* (National Textbook Co., 1988), David Thomas notes: "What debaters need is a unique glossary of words and phrases important to an understanding of debate theory." What debaters also need are clear and easy-to-understand definitions, examples or applications of debate terms, and—perhaps most important—examples of how debaters actually use the terms.

NTC's Dictionary of Debate meets these needs. It offers a complete compilation of all the terms debaters, coaches, judges, and debate theorists will want to see. Each term is defined in simple, plain English. The *Dictionary* gives full examples of nearly all terms, so debaters can see what the words mean when applied. The *Dictionary* also gives examples of how the terms are used in debates or in conversations and writing about debate. Cross-references are included so users can see how the terms interrelate. Each of these characteristics is unique to *NTC's Dictionary of Debate*.

The world of debate is exciting. *NTC's Dictionary of Debate* offers an entry into the excitement through its complete treatment of debate terms and use of clear definitions and examples. It eliminates the mysteries of debate jargon. *NTC's Dictionary of Debate* makes sense.

HOW TO USE
THIS DICTIONARY

1. Main entries are printed in boldface type. If a term, such as **impromptu,** has more than one distinct meaning, these meanings are defined in separate, numbered entries for ease in cross-referencing.

2. *Definitions,* in clear, easy-to-understand language, follow main entry heads.

3. *Examples* provide further clarification for most terms. Examples not only show how terms are applied, but also offer outlines, mini-debates, and illustrations to make sure concepts and techniques are clearly conveyed and understood.

4. *Usage* subentries show how terms are actually used by debaters. Everyday English translations of debate jargon are given in parentheses after each usage example.

5. *Synonyms* are provided when a basic term or concept is known by more than one label. Many synonyms appear under separate entries to explain distinctions made between similar terms.

6. *Antonyms* are provided for appropriate main entries. Most antonyms appear under separate entries.

7. Cross-references are provided for nearly every entry under the subhead *See also.* The network of cross-references provides further insight into related terms and concepts.

ABOUT THE AUTHOR

Jim Hanson began his forensics career in high school and was a state quarterfinalist in policy debate. As a debate coach, he led his John F. Kennedy High School (Seattle) team to the 1984 state AAA championship. As a competitor for Western Washington University, Jim won over 100 awards. He and his partner took fifth place at the 1987 Cross-Examination Debate Association National Championship.

Hanson is currently coach of Interlake High School's speech and debate team. He is a graduate teaching assistant in the speech communication department at the University of Washington, working toward a doctorate degree. Coauthor with Susan L. Kline and Dee Oseroff-Varnell of a Western Speech Communication Association top competitive panel paper, "Learning to Argue: Developmental Shifts in Deductive Reasoning and Argument Analysis," he also is author of an upcoming debate textbook, *Breaking Down Barriers: How to Debate* (1989).

Hanson is a staff member of the Seattle Debate Workshop and the Western Washington Debate Institute.

A

absolute

Definition: Completely; totally; 100 percent.

Example: Not one country is sold repressive weapons.

Usage: That's an absolute argument. *(The argument completely proves a point or beats the opponent's case.)*

See also: ABSOLUTE SOLVENCY

absolute solvency

Definition: The plan completely solves or completely does not solve a problem.

Example: "Their plan will not help one single person" is an *absolute solvency* argument. "Our plan will completely solve the toxic dumping problem" is an argument that shows *absolute solvency.*

Usage: I ran an absolute solvency argument. *(I argued that their plan would not gain any advantage.)* We gain an absolute advantage. *(We totally solve the problem.)*

See also: ABSOLUTE

academic debate

Definition: A school activity where students engage in debate by forming two opposing sides. The two students on each side try to persuade a judge or panel of judges to support their side of an issue.

Example: In *academic debate,* two teams compete against each other at tournaments. The tournaments are held at high schools and colleges. A mini-debate on the resolution "RESOLVED: That the United States should ban alcohol" might look like this:

Affirmative: Banning alcohol would help reduce alcoholism and drunken driving.

Negative: Banning alcohol would not reduce alcoholism or drunken driving because people would turn to the black market and then organized crime would grow.

See also: AFFIRMATIVE, ARGUMENT (2), AUDIENCE DEBATE, DEBATE, DEBATE FORMATS, NEGATIVE, PUBLIC DEBATE

ad hominem attack
Definition: An attack against a person, instead of against that person's arguments.
Example: "John, our opponent, once again tries to make a good argument, but, as usual, fails."
Usage: Team X made ad hominems. *(Team X attacked their opponents and not their opponents' arguments.)*
See also: FALLACY

ad populum fallacy
See: BANDWAGON FALLACY

add-on
See: ADD-ON ADVANTAGE

add-on advantage
Definition: An advantage presented in the second affirmative or second negative constructive that shows a plan or counterplan will gain benefits in addition to those already presented.
Example: In the first affirmative speech, a debater might argue that her plan would decrease unemployment. The second affirmative speaker might present an *add-on advantage* by showing that the plan would also decrease inflation.

Usage: I will present additive advantages to our counterplan. *(I, the second negative speaker, will show other benefits to the counterplan that my partner presented.)* I have two add-ons for our plan. *(I will present two new advantages of our plan that were not mentioned in the first affirmative speech.)* Each turnaround is an added advantage for the affirmative. *(The turned around disadvantages actually favor the affirmative plan and should be considered additional advantages for the affirmative plan.)*

Synonyms: ADDED ADVANTAGE, ADDITIVE ADVANTAGE, ADD-ON

See also: ADVANTAGE

added advantage

See: ADD-ON ADVANTAGE

additive advantage

See: ADD-ON ADVANTAGE

adjustment and repairs case

See: MINOR REPAIR

administer

Definition: The act of running a program or policy. An affirmative team will have their plan administered by a group of people.

Usage: Our plan will be administered by a seven-member board. *(Our plan will be run by a seven-member board.)*

See also: ADMINISTRATION, BOARD

administration

Definition: The organized group of people in charge of a program or policy.

Example: The Reagan *administration* was in control of U.S. policy.

Usage: The current administration is not doing anything about this problem. *(The group of people in charge aren't doing anything to solve the problem.)*

See also: ADMINISTER, AGENT OF ACTION/CHANGE, BOARD

administrator of debate

Definition: The person who organizes and manages a debate team.

Usage: He's the administrator. *(He's the person who organizes and manages a debate team.)*

See also: COACH, DIRECTOR OF DEBATE

advantage

Definition: A reason to take a course of action; to show a plan will offer a benefit. An advantage usually includes significance, inherency, and solvency.

Example: An affirmative might argue that a plan to increase pollution control devices would gain this *advantage:*

    I. Pollution control devices would save lives.

        A. (Significance) Pollution is killing many people.

        B. (Inherency) Current pollution control is inadequate.

        C. (Solvency) Pollution control would prevent deaths.

Usage: We ran a human rights advantage. *(We argued that our plan would reduce human rights abuses.)* We showed the disadvantage would actually be an advantage to our plan. *(We showed that our plan would actually gain a benefit, an advantage—not a disadvantage as our opponents had argued.)*

See also: BENEFIT, DISADVANTAGE, INHERENCY, PLAN, SIGNIFICANCE, SOLVENCY

advocate

Definition: (*n.*) A person who tries to persuade others to agree with a position. (*v.*) To try to persuade others to agree with a position.

Example: Debaters are *advocates (n.)* because they try to persuade their judges. Debaters *advocate (v.)* new policies and values when they try to persuade their judges.

Usage: We advocate a national health insurance program. *(We support and urge you also to support national health insurance.)*

See also: ARGUE, DEBATE

affirmative

Definition: The side that supports the resolution in a debate.

Example: The *affirmative* would support the resolution "RESOLVED: That the parliamentary system is superior to the executive system" by arguing for the parliamentary system over the executive system. The *affirmative* might support the resolution "RESOLVED: That the United States should significantly change its Central American policy" by arguing for increased food aid in Central America.

Usage: What's your affirmative? *(When you are debating on the affirmative, what is your case?)* They're good on the affirmative. *(When they support the resolution in debates, that team does very well.)*

See also: NEGATIVE, RESOLUTION

affirmative case

Definition: The arguments an affirmative team presents to support the resolution.

Example: An *affirmative case* that supports the resolution "RE-SOLVED: That the United States should increase space exploration" might show that sending a space station to Venus would increase available minerals for the world's use. An *affirmative case* supporting the resolution "RESOLVED: That AIDS testing is justified" might show that AIDS cases are rising and since testing would help reduce AIDS, the tests are justified.

Usage: What's their affirmative case? *(What position does that team take and what arguments do they use to support the resolution?)*

Note: "Case" is often used interchangeably with the term "Plan."

See also: ADVANTAGE, CASE, NEGATIVE BLOCK, PLAN, VALUE SUPPORT

agenda setting

See: ISSUE

agent

Definition: The subject of the resolution.

Example: The *agent* of the resolution "RESOLVED: That the federal government should increase affirmative action programs" would be "the federal government" because it is the subject of the resolution.

See also: AGENT COUNTERPLAN, AGENT OF ACTION/CHANGE, VALUE OBJECT

agent counterplan

Definition: A negative plan that supports a different agent from the agent in the resolution.

Example: An affirmative team supports the resolution "RE-SOLVED: That the federal government should change criminal trial rules." The negative could argue in support of an *agent counterplan* to dissolve the federal government and switch to a world government; or the negative could urge the *agent counterplan* that the states, not the federal government, should change criminal trial rules.

See also: AGENT, COUNTERPLAN

agent of action/change

Definition: The part of the plan that is responsible for the change supported by the affirmative; the board.

Usage: What is the agent of change in your plan? *(Who will be implementing your plan? Who will be putting your plan into action?)*

See also: ADMINISTRATION, BOARD

aggressive

Definition: To be hostile and pushy.

Example: An *aggressive* debater might act overbearing during cross-examination and attempt to belittle her opponents.

Usage: He's a really aggressive speaker. *(He's really pushy and hostile when he debates.)*

See also: ARGUMENTATIVE, ASSERTIVENESS

agreement

Definition: Occurs when two sides concur on an argument or a position.

Example: There would be *agreement* in a debate if the affirmative and negative both felt that there was a serious problem.

Antonym: DISAGREEMENT

See also: DISCUSSION

alphabetical filing system

Definition: To place evidence cards or briefs into sections with titles that are arranged in alphabetical order.

Example: An *alphabetical filing system* might include, in order, the following categories: Discrimination, Health care, Housing,

Medicare, Retirement, Social Security; evidence cards or briefs would be placed into each category.

See also: BRIEF, CARD, FILE

alternate causality

Definition: A factor, not originally considered, which is actually the cause (or one of the causes) of an event.

Example: An *alternate causality* to the causal argument "Coal burning causes acid rain" might be "Automobile exhaust actually is the main factor causing acid rain."

See also: ASSOCIATION, BRINK, REASONING

alternative

See: VALUE ALTERNATIVE

alternative justification case

Definition: An affirmative case that includes several plans, each having independent advantages.

Example: An *alternative justification case* might argue for a plan that closes down nuclear power plants, increases solar power, and bans oil imports. The advantages to the plan might be 1) closing nuclear plants would decrease hazardous nuclear waste, 2) increasing solar power would provide environmentally safe energy, and 3) banning oil imports would decrease U.S. dependence on foreign oil and thereby decrease the chance of gas shortages.

Usage: They ran an alternative justification case and severed advantage two. *(They argued a case with several plans, and they dropped the part of the plan that gained advantage two—probably because their opponents showed that that part of the plan caused a large disadvantage.*

See also: AFFIRMATIVE CASE, CONDITIONALITY, DISCO, SEVER

ambiguous

Definition: Lack of clarity; vague.

Example: An *ambiguous* plan might support a change in military spending. This plan is *ambiguous* because it is unclear what military spending will be changed and how much change will occur.

Usage: Their position on nuclear weapons is ambiguous. *(The other team is not clear on whether they support or reject nuclear weapons.)*

See also: VAGUE, VOID FOR VAGUENESS

amend

Definition: A change in a plan or case made after the plan or case has been presented.

Example: The affirmative presents a plan that will be financed by a gas and income tax. Then, after the negative presents a disadvantage against the gas tax, the affirmative team *amends* the plan by funding the plan only through the income tax.

Usage: We amended our case by getting rid of the privacy argument. *(In order to avoid the value objections run against the privacy argument, we no longer supported the privacy argument.)* We amended our plan in the 1AR. *(In the first affirmative rebuttal speech we changed our plan.)*

See also: DISCO, SEVER

American Forensic Association

Definition: An organization of directors of forensics and interested teachers, professors, and students in American schools and colleges that promotes the study and practice of argumentation.

See also: FORENSICS, NATIONAL FORENSIC LEAGUE

analogy

Definition: A comparison of two items or events.

Example: U.S. involvement in Nicaragua is like Vietnam.

Usage: Sweden's success with health care insurance would be analogous to what would happen in America. *(America would have the same success with health care insurance as Sweden.)*

See also: REASONING

analysis

Definition: Coming up with points that will prove a main point or case.

Example: An *analysis* of the argument "Dogs are dangerous" might include coming up with these points: 1) Pit bulls have killed; 2) runaway dogs are health threats; and 3) dogs running loose are road hazards.

Usage:	Let's analyze this argument. *(Let's take a closer look at this argument to find points that will develop a case.)* The analysis is really good in that case. *(That case is strongly supported by sharp, clear, and important points.)*
See also:	ANALYTICAL, DEDUCTION, ISSUE, SUBORDINATION

analytical

Definition:	Having the ability to analyze.
Example:	A person who carefully studied issues and was able to come up with important points would be called *analytical*.
See also:	ANALYSIS, DEDUCTION

answer

Definition:	Response to questions or opposing arguments.
Example:	During cross-examination, the questioner might ask, "Is freedom more important than life?" An *answer* might be, "It can be when people have very little freedom." During a speech, a speaker might *answer* opponent arguments by saying, "I have two answers to my opponent's argument. First, a jobs program would not cost that much. Estimates show it will cost just $8 billion. Second, in the long run it saves money because it gets people off welfare."
Usage:	She had really good answers to that argument. *(She made good responses to that argument.)* Their answers in cross-ex are really bad. *(Their responses to questions in cross-examination are poor.)*
See also:	CROSS-EXAMINATION, RESPONSE

anticipatory argument/refutation

See:	PREEMPTION

appeal

Definition:	To make an argument that is supported by the audience's or judge's beliefs.
Example:	An *appeal* to a judge's belief in the value of life might be, "The values of democracy help insure the quality of life and will even save lives."
See also:	PATHOS, SOPHISTRY

argue

Definition: To offer reasons for or against a position.

Example: A debater who says, "School prayer is good because it allows students to express their religion," is *arguing*.

Usage: What did you argue? *(What arguments did you present to support your case?)*

See also: ARGUMENT, REASONING, RESPOND

arguing in a circle

Definition: To support an assertion with a reason that is the assertion itself.

Example: The death penalty is an effective deterrent because it scares people and it scares people because it is an effective deterrent.

See also: BEGGING THE QUESTION, FALLACY

argument (1)

Definition: A claim supported by evidence.

Example: Cars are dangerous because they get into accidents.

See also: EVIDENCE, LABEL, RESPONSE

argument (2)

Definition: A dispute; a debate.

Example: Jerry Falwell and Jesse Jackson debating whether the United States should divest from South Africa are engaged in an *argument (2)*.

Usage: They had a big argument about the taxes in cross-examination. *(Two debaters disputed a tax issue during the questioning period.)*

See also: DEBATE, DISPUTE

argument by argument debate

Definition: A debate in which just one issue is argued at a time.

Example: On a resolution "RESOLVED: That drug testing should be given to all workers," an *argument by argument debate* would have debaters argue just one issue; for example, "Is there a drug abuse problem?" The issue that the debaters argue is usually an argument presented in an affirmative case. After that issue or argument has been thoroughly dealt with, the debaters go on to the next argument in the case.

Usage: Let's have an argument by argument debate. *(Let's have a debate where we deal with one issue at a time.)*

See also: DEBATE FORMATS, REFUTATION

argument field

Definition: Occurs when arguments are accepted because of similar backing.

Example: The court arguments "Drug testing violates the Fourth Amendment because it involves direct observation of private activities" and "Drug testing violates the Fourth Amendment because it involves an assumption of guilty before innocent" may be from the same *argument field* if the two are similarly backed. For example, both arguments may be backed by court precedents that require private activities to be given the presumption of innocence because of the Fourth Amendment's stand against unreasonable search and seizure.

Synonym: FIELD (1)

See also: BACKING, FIELD DEPENDENCE, FIELD INDEPENDENCE, TOULMIN MODEL OF ARGUMENT

argumentation

Definition: The process of reason-giving by people seeking to justify positions.

Example: The reasons Reagan gave for his tax cuts and the reasons opponents gave against his tax cuts.

Usage: I study argumentation. *(I look at reasons people give for their positions.)*

See also: DEBATE, DIALECTIC, PERSUASION, RHETORIC, SOPHISTRY

Argumentation and Advocacy

Definition: Journal of the American Forensic Association. A publication that includes articles on the practice and theory of debate, argumentation, and advocacy theory.

See also: CEDA YEARBOOK

argumentative

Definition: To frequently want to dispute or debate others.

Example: Harold and Suzy argue about everything. They are very *argumentative.*

See also: AGGRESSIVE

artificial competition

Definition: To add extraneous elements to a counterplan or value alternative that would be undesirable or impossible to implement with extraneous elements of a plan or value object.

Example: An *artificially competitive* counterplan might be one that takes the money which would fund the plan. This is *artificially competitive* because, while it would be undesirable and perhaps even impossible to implement this funding mechanism with the plan, this type of funding is extraneous—it is not necessary. It would not be undesirable, nor impossible, to implement the plan and counterplan with a different funding mechanism. *Artificial competitiveness* is usually considered illegitimate because the essential elements of the plan and counterplan, or alternative and value object, are still not competitive.

See also: COMPETITION (1), COUNTERPLAN, VALUE ALTERNATIVE

assertion

Definition: A statement or argument without noticeable support.

Example: "Airplanes are dangerous" is an *assertion* until it is supported.

Usage: They kept asserting that their plan would solve. *(They argued throughout the debate that their plan would solve the problem without ever proving it.)*

See also: CLAIM

assertiveness

Definition: Confidently presenting one's arguments without being rude.

Example: Deana presents her arguments confidently, is able to make her point, and is still courteous. She is *assertive.*

See also: AGGRESSIVE

association

Definition: Two events that are related to each other.

Example: Cigarette smoking is *associated* with cancer because cigarette smokers get more cancers.

Usage: They only showed an association. *(They did not prove one thing caused another—just that the two occurred at the same time.)*

See also: CAUSAL LINK, CAUSATION, CORRELATION, LINK

assumption

Definition: An unstated premise of an argument; what an argument presumes to be true to make its conclusion valid; a warrant.

Example: If a person states that a radio could kill a human by electrocution, that person is making the *assumption* that a radio has enough electric current to cause a deadly electrocution.

Usage: Doesn't your argument assume that companies won't leave the country? *(Doesn't your argument presume that companies won't leave the country?)*

See also: ENTHYMEME, PREMISE, PRESUMPTION, SYLLOGISM

attack and defense

See: REBUTTAL, REFUTATION

attitudinal inherency

Definition: The attitudes of those in charge of current programs and policies that prevent or help a solution to a problem or an achievement of an advantage.

Example: A mini-debate about *attitudinal inherency.*

Affirmative: The current administration is against changing the Israeli embassy location, thereby making diplomatic efforts useless.

Negative: The current administration is making realistic efforts to persuade Israel to deal with its embassy location. This is the best diplomatic effort America can make.

Usage: They used attitudinal inherency. *(Instead of discussing laws, programs, or policies as the main emphasis of their inherency, they used the attitudes of the government.)*

See also: INHERENCY, STRUCTURAL INHERENCY

audience

Definition: The person or persons listening to speakers in a debate.

Example: The judge and any other observers of a debate are an *audience.*

Usage: We adapted to the audience. *(We presented our arguments in a favorable way to the people listening to the debate.)*

See also: AUDIENCE ANALYSIS, CRITIC, JUDGE

audience analysis

Definition: The process of finding out what the audience likes to hear from speakers.

Example: Finding out that the judge in your debate round wants you to speak slower and likes criteria arguments is *audience analysis.*

See also: AUDIENCE, BELIEF, JUDGE

audience debate

Definition: A debate for a large group of people.

Example: A debate in front of the Rotary Club would be an *audience debate.*

See also: DEBATE

authority

Definition: Someone with power, prestige, or expertise in a certain field.

Example: Henry Kissinger is an *authority* on foreign policy.

Usage: What authority did you quote on that point? *(What expert did you quote to support that argument?)*

See also: EVIDENCE, EXPERT, SOURCE

B

backing

Definition: The support for the warrant of an argument; the support that shows that the evidence proves the claim.

Example: Evidence: Many prisons are more than fifty years old and in disrepair.
Warrant: Since old prisons are in disrepair, they need repair.
Backing: Because without repairing the prisons, security risks increase,
Claim: therefore, prisons need repair.

Usage: What is the backing for that argument? *(What proves that you have supported your argument well?)*

See also: CLAIM, EVIDENCE, TOULMIN MODEL OF ARGUMENT, WARRANT

backlash

Definition: An angry reaction to a new policy.

Example: Right-wing death squads in El Salvador would *backlash* against a U.S. aid cutoff by killing thousands.

Usage: They ran an elitist backlash disadvantage against us. *(They argued that elite, or ruling, classes would angrily react against our plan.)*

See also: DISADVANTAGE, VALUE OBJECTION

baiting (an opponent)

Definition: Enticing an opponent into making an argument that one can easily defeat.

Example: Debater Y might *bait an opponent* by pushing that opponent to agree to decrease military spending. Debater Y could then use arguments prepared ahead of time that say decreased military spending is bad.

Usage: They're trying to bait us. *(They're trying to get us to make an argument that they can easily beat.)*

See also: RED HERRING, SEVERING, SKELETON

ballot

Definition: The sheet of paper upon which a judge writes his or her decision.

Example:

AMERICAN FORENSIC ASSOCIATION DEBATE BALLOT   FORM E

Division _____ Round _____ Room _____ Date _____ Judge _____

Affirmative # _____ School _____ Negative # _____ School _____

Rate all speakers and both teams on a scale from 30 (Superior) to 1 (Poor)
Rank each debater in order of excellence (1st for best, 2nd for next best, etc.)

Rankings must be consistent with ratings; ties in rank are not permitted.

1st Aff. _____   1st Neg. _____
        (Name)   (Name)

2nd Aff. _____   2nd Neg. _____
        (Name)   (Name)

Aff. TEAM rating . . . . _____ Neg. TEAM rating . . . . _____
   (Teams should be rated on a 30-point scale; do NOT total individual speaker points.)

COMMENTS AND BASIS FOR DECISION:

In my opinion, this debate was won by _____ representing _____
                                    (Aff. or Neg.)   (School and/or #)

_____   _____
(Judge's name)   (School)

COPYRIGHT, AMERICAN FORENSIC ASSOCIATION, 1974

Usage: We got the ballot. *(The judge gave us the·victory on the ballot.)* Did you see the ballot? *(Did you see what the judge wrote on the ballot?)*

See also: DECISION, JUDGE

bandwagon fallacy

Definition: To support an argument by showing that everyone else agrees with the argument.

Example: Capital punishment is obviously good since polls show most Americans support it.

Usage: The affirmative argument showing people support the United Nations is a bandwagon fallacy. *(The affirmative is relying on popular opinion rather than solid evidence and logical argument to support the United Nations.)*

Synonym: AD POPULUM FALLACY

See also: FALLACY

barrier

Definition: An attitude, law, program, or policy that prevents the present system from solving the problem or achieving the advantage.

Example: Laws that allow toxic waste dumping into landfills will never solve the cancers caused by toxic wastes. There is a *barrier* to the laws solving the problem.

Usage: What is the barrier to your plan? *(What prevents your plan from being enacted?)*

Synonym: INHERENT BARRIER

See also: CASESIDE BARRIER, INHERENCY, PLANSIDE BARRIER, SHOULD-COULD FALLACY

begging the question

Definition: To support a claim with the claim itself.

Example: Health programs are good because health programs are good.

Usage: He begged the question with his "Vietnam War was good" argument. *(He argued that the Vietnam War was good because it was good.)*

See also: ARGUING IN A CIRCLE, FALLACY, QUESTION BEGGING

beginner's division
See: NOVICE DIVISION

belief
Definition: The positions, ideas, or thoughts one agrees with.
Example: Two *beliefs* are "I agree that the freeway should be widened" and "I feel that helping the poor is a good idea."
See also: APPEAL, AUDIENCE ANALYSIS, OPINION, PATHOS, PRESUMPTION

benefit
Definition: An advantage; the desirable result of a value or policy.
Example: The United Nations provides numerous *benefits,* like preventing some wars and feeding the poor. The value of liberty *benefits* people because it gives them the opportunity to improve themselves.
Usage: The value's benefits outweigh its costs. *(The desirable results of the value outweigh the harmful results and therefore the value should be considered good.)*
See also: ADVANTAGE, HARMS, PROBLEM, VALUE SUPPORT

benefits case
See: NET BENEFITS CASE

best definition
Definition: The highest quality definition; a topicality standard that advocates choosing just one definition of a word (the best definition).
Example: If a team argues that legal definitions are best, other dictionary definitions, even though reasonable, would not be acceptable.
Usage: Use the best definition standard. *(Choose one definition, the best one, instead of allowing the affirmative to have a reasonable definition.)*
See also: DEFINITION, REASONABLE STANDARD, TOPICALITY

bias
Definition: To favor a style of debating, types of arguments, or positions on issues.
Example: A judge's *bias* might favor the negative side of the resolution. An author may have a *bias* in favor of conservative ideas.

Usage: That judge has a bias toward liberal policies. *(That judge favors liberal policies, and hence debaters need to adapt to those biases.)*
See also: BIASED, PRESUMPTION

biased
Definition: Favoritism toward one side or toward one position on an issue for reasons unrelated to logical argument; a source's favoritism because of a vested interest.
Example: A *biased* judge votes for a certain team no matter what. A tobacco spokesperson that argued that cigarettes don't cause cancer would be *biased* because that spokesperson is paid to make such statements.
Usage: That judge is biased. *(That judge is unfair and votes for teams he or she likes, instead of voting based upon the arguments the teams present.)* The source is biased. *(The source made this argument because he or she personally gains from making the argument.)*
See also: BIAS, INTERVENTION

bibliography
Definition: A listing of sources, like books, journals, and newspapers, for finding information and evidence on an issue.
Example: The beginning of a toxic waste *bibliography:*
Belfiglio, J. (1981). "Hazardous Wastes: Preserving the Nuisance Remedy." Stanford law review, 33, 675–91.
Buckley, C.H. (1985). "A Suggested Remedy for Toxic Injury: Class Actions, Epidemiology, and Economic Efficiency." William and Mary law review, 26, 497–543.
Carno, T. (1984). "A New Cause of Action for Massive Medical Toxic Injury." Glendale law review, 6, 15–29.
See also: EVIDENCE, RESEARCH

bidirectionality
Definition: The issue of whether the resolution allows the affirmative to both increase or decrease an action.
Example: The affirmative would interpret the topic "RESOLVED: That the United States should increase space development" *bidirectionally* if they supported a plan which increased space development by increasing the development of zones in space that ban military activity.

Usage: We argued bidirectionality is unfair. *(We argued that the affirmative's interpretation of the topic allowed for both increases and decreases and therefore eroded negative ground for debate.)*

See also: DEBATABILITY, GROUND (1), RESOLUTION, TOPICALITY

big impact argument
See: MEGA-IMPACT ARGUMENT

bloc
See: NEGATIVE BLOCK

block
Definition: A stack of evidence organized by an outline.
Example: An outline of a block:
1. Arms control increases risk of war. (evidence cards 1–6)
2. Arms control does not stop more weapons. (cards 7–10)
3. Arms control causes new weapons. (cards 11–12)
4. Arms control creates imbalance in weapons. (cards 13–16)
5. Imbalance in weapons causes nuclear war. (cards 17–18)

Usage: We ran a block against that team. *(We made a series of structured arguments against that team's case.)*

See also: BRIEF, EVIDENCE

board
Definition: The group of people that the affirmative says will run the affirmative plan.
Example: "The affirmative will establish a seven-member, munificently salaried board to implement the affirmative mandates."

See also: ADMINISTRATION, PLAN, PLANK

body language
Definition: The communication made by one's body movements.
Example: Tony's slouching posture made him look unprofessional to some judges. Sheila's wild arm gestures made her look too excited and out of control. Jana's poise and calm appearance made her look in control.

Usage: His body language makes him look nervous. *(He looked nervous because of the way he moved or held his body.)*

See also: COMMUNICATION, DELIVERY, GESTURES

bombast

Definition: The use of excited voice, body movements, or emotional appeals without reason to support an argument.

Example: A speaker yelling and pleading indignantly, "This is wrong! Is it not the height of what is wrong? Indeed it is!"

See also: APPEAL, FALLACY, PATHOS

book

Definition: Bound, written pages that usually tell a story or address an issue.

Example: *Decision by Debate* is a *book* by Douglas Ehninger and Wayne Brockriede.

See also: GOVERNMENT DOCUMENTS, PERIODICALS, RESEARCH

brainstorming

Definition: Coming up with points, arguments, positions, and issues by open-mindedly thinking by yourself or with others.

See also: ANALYSIS

break

Definition: To have a good enough win-loss record at a tournament to qualify for the finals rounds.

Example: After going 5–1 in preliminary debate rounds, team L12 *broke* to finals.

Usage: Did you break? *(Did you have a good enough record to make it to finals rounds?)*

See also: ELIMINATION ROUNDS, IN, OUT

brief

Definition: A sheet of paper with arguments on one issue.

Example: A sample brief appears on page 22.

See also: ARGUMENT, CARD, EVIDENCE, FILE

(M2)

1. <u>INCREASE</u> IN WEAPONS ↑ PROLIFERATION

    Gerard Smith, C. Smith, Consultants International Group,
    NUCLEAR NONPROLIFERATION POLICY, Senate Hearings, Committee
    on Governmental Affairs, June 24, 1981, p. 49

    As we increase our nuclear forces we may well be increasing the
    difficulty of keeping nuclear weapons out of the hands of other
    countries. Our example is a more potent lever to control spread
    than even safeguards and export controls.

2. THERE IS A DIRECT LINK

    Olof Palme, Nuclear War, Nuclear Proliferation & Their Con-
    sequences, 1986, p. 27

    There is indeed a direct connection between the threat of
    proliferation and the dangers of deterrence ~~which I was talking
    about earlier.~~ The nuclear-weapon States are in effect saying
    that they can achieve security by building nuclear weapons, that
    they can gain political advantage and that they can also prevent
    war.

3. ↑ PROLIFERATION OF THRESHOLD COUNTRIES

    Maxwell Stanley, Hearings Foreign Relations, Nov. 13, '81,
    p. 38

    Superpower emphasis on strategic weapons encourages the further
    proliferation of nuclear weapons among threshold countries and
    stimulates the buildup of conventional weapons. Because there
    is no guarantee that greater military power will assure peace,
    the security of all nations, including the United States, con-
    tinues in jeopardy.

4. STRONG CONNECTION

    Michael Nacht, Prof. of Nat. Sec. U Maryland, The Age of Vulner-
    ability, 1985, p. 167

    It has long been argued, particularly by citizens of less developed
    countries, that there is a strong connection between vertical
    proliferation--the continued growth of the nuclear arsenals of
    the United States and the soviet Union--and horizontal prolifera-
    tion--the spread of nuclear weapons to nonnuclear states.

5. US/USSR RACE IS THE PRIMARY POLIF. MOTIVE

    Olof Palme, Common Security: A Blueprint for Survival, 1982, p. 16

    The primary impetus behind the continuing proliferation of
    nuclear weapons is the competition between the United States and
    the Soviet Union. Together they probably account for about 95
    percent of the world's nuclear arsenals.

brink

Definition: The point at which something occurs; the threshold.

Example: Daryl will get the groceries if you give him two dollars; if you give him any less, he won't do it. The *brink,* then, is at two dollars because that is the point when Daryl will act. Congress won't pass protectionist legislation until the trade imbalance gets to $18 billion. The point at which the trade imbalance hits $18 billion is the *brink.*

Usage: They argued no brink against our nuclear war disadvantage. *(They argued that there was no point at which nuclear war would occur.)*

Synonym: THRESHOLD

See also: DISADVANTAGE

British format debate

Definition: A type of debate used mainly in Great Britain and its former colonies that emphasizes audience participation, humor, and speaker analysis. During a British format debate, the speakers present their arguments in front of an audience. The audience may interrupt a speaker with a comment or question. The speakers use lots of humor, logical reasoning, and little quoted evidence.

Synonym: PARLIAMENTARY DEBATE

See also: DEBATE FORMATS

burden of communication

Definition: The obligation to clearly express arguments and positions.

Example: Speaking too rapidly for a judge or speaking unclearly would be a failure of the *burden of communication.* Debaters who speak in a pleasing and easy to understand manner for a judge meet their *burden of communication.*

See also: COMMUNICATION, DELIVERY, STYLE

burden of going forward

Definition: The process of meeting one's burden of rejoinder.

See: BURDEN OF REJOINDER

burden of proof

Definition: The obligation to prove a claim or a proposition.
Example: Since most judges feel that the affirmative must prove the resolution, the affirmative has the *burden of proof.* A debater who claimed that the death penalty is racist would have a *burden of proof,* a need to prove her claim.
Usage: They have the burden of proof. *(They need to prove their case.)*
See also: BURDEN OF REBUTTAL, BURDEN OF REJOINDER, BUR-DEN OF THE AFFIRMATIVE, BURDEN OF THE NEGATIVE, PRESUMPTION

burden of rebuttal

Definition: The obligation to solidly rebuild one's case by responding to attacks against that case and by reestablishing the case's validity.
Example: A debater who meets his *burden of rebuttal* might state: "In our case we argued that rivers are polluted. Our opponent responded by quoting a chemical company manager who said only a few rivers are polluted. First, their source is bi-ased. The manager's company pollutes, and he's just speaking for profit. Second, more and more rivers are be-ing polluted. According to...."
Usage: The negative failed to meet its burden of rebuttal. *(The negative did not answer arguments against its case or did not rebuild its original case.)*
Synonym: ATTACK AND DEFENSE
See also: BURDEN OF PROOF, BURDEN OF REJOINDER, BURDEN OF THE AFFIRMATIVE, BURDEN OF THE NEGATIVE

burden of refutation

See: BURDEN OF REJOINDER

burden of rejoinder

Definition: The obligation to solidly respond to opponent arguments.
Example: A debater who meets her *burden of rejoinder* might state: "In the B point in their case, the affirmative claimed that nu-clear power plants would increase energy production. I will have two arguments. First, nuclear power plants produce little energy. According to...."

Usage: The affirmative failed to meet its burden of rejoinder on the value objection. *(The affirmative did not give solid answers in response to the value objection.)*

Synonyms: BURDEN OF GOING FORWARD, BURDEN OF REFUTATION

See also: BURDEN OF PROOF, BURDEN OF REBUTTAL, BURDEN OF THE AFFIRMATIVE, BURDEN OF THE NEGATIVE, DEFENSE

burden of the affirmative

Definition: The affirmative team's obligation, at the end of the debate, to present a case the judge finds convincing enough to vote for the affirmative.

Example: A judge will vote affirmative if the affirmative can show that their plan will save 250 lives. To show that the plan saves 250 lives is the *burden of the affirmative.*

See also: BURDEN OF PROOF, BURDEN OF REBUTTAL, BURDEN OF REJOINDER, BURDEN OF THE NEGATIVE, PRESUMPTION

burden of the negative

Definition: The negative team's obligation, at the end of the debate, to present a case the judge finds convincing enough to vote for the negative.

Example: The judge will vote negative if the negative can show that the present system is superior to the affirmative plan. The *burden of the negative,* then, is to show the present system is superior.

See also: BURDEN OF PROOF, BURDEN OF REBUTTAL, BURDEN OF REJOINDER, BURDEN OF THE AFFIRMATIVE, PRE-SUMPTION

bye

Definition: Occurs when a team is not scheduled to debate another team. A team is given a bye when there is an odd number of teams in a division. The posting will show each team that will hit each other and it will show the one team that receives a bye. The team with the bye does not debate any-one, but receives a "win" for its record. Usually, a team that receives a bye in later rounds is not doing well.

Usage: Did you have a bye last round? *(Were you scheduled for no debate last round?)*

See also: FORFEIT, NO SHOW, WIN

CEDA (Cross-Examination Debate Association)

Definition: An organization of college debate teams that debate the CEDA resolution (usually a value or quasi-policy resolution). Schools accumulate one point for each win of the top three teams debating at a tournament.

See also: CEDA DEBATE, NDT DEBATE

CEDA debate

Definition: College debate using the CEDA resolution (usually a value or quasi-policy topic).

See also: CEDA, NDT DEBATE

CEDA National Championship

Definition: Established in 1986, this tournament features CEDA debate teams from across the United States. The team that wins the tournament is declared the CEDA national champion.

See also: NATIONAL DEBATE TOURNAMENT

CEDA Yearbook

Definition: A journal featuring articles on the theory and practice of debate in CEDA

See also: ARGUMENTATION AND ADVOCACY

camp

Definition: A place where debaters go to learn about debate, usually during the summer. Camps usually last two to five weeks and include theory lectures and debate practice.

Example: The American Debate Institute and the Seattle Debate Workshop are *camps.*

Usage: What camp are you going to this summer? *(What place are you going to this summer to learn about debate?)*

Synonym: INSTITUTE

capture

Definition: To claim the advantages or support from the noncompetitive and topical portions of the opponent's counterplan or value alternative.

Example: The affirmative *captured* the negative national health care counterplan and claimed its cost savings. The affirmative supported a plan for preventive medicine. They argued that the negative national health care counterplan is topical and that national health care is not competitive because the government should use preventive medicine in the national health care program. Since the negative had argued that preventive medicine was too costly but had also argued that its national health care counterplan saved a lot of money, the affirmative avoided the cost disadvantage by *capturing* the counterplan and its cost savings.

See also: COMPETITIVENESS, COUNTERPLAN, EXTRA-COMPETITIVENESS, PERMUTATION.

card

Definition: A $3'' \times 5''$ or $4'' \times 6''$ index card with evidence on it.

Example: A sample card appears on page 28.

Usage: We outcarded them. *(We used more evidence than they did.)*
That's a really good card. *(That is a good piece of evidence.)*

See also: BRIEF, EVIDENCE, FILE

> James R. Knickman and Nelda McCall. "A Pre-
> paid Managed Approach to Long-Term Care."
> HEALTH AFFAIRS, Spring 1986, p. 90
>
> "In 1984, nursing home expenditures totaled $32
> billion, an increase of 11.1 percent over the previous
> year."

card catalog
Definition: A listing of all the books in the library.
See also: INDEX, INFOTRACK

cardfile
Definition: An organized collection of evidence on index cards, usually in a filebox.
See also: BRIEF, EVIDENCE, FILE

case
Definition: An organized and persuasive series of arguments for or against the resolution.
Usage: What case are they running? *(What main arguments do they give for the resolution?)* This case is good. *(This series of arguments for the resolution is very good.)*
See also: ADVANTAGE, AFFIRMATIVE CASE, CASE STRUCTURES, NEGATIVE BLOCK, VALUE SUPPORT

case construction

Definition: Researching, organizing, and writing a persuasive series of arguments for or against the resolution.

Usage: Let's construct our case. *(Let's put together our arguments.)*

See also: CASE, CASE STRUCTURES

case structures

Definition: Different ways of organizing an affirmative case.

Example: There are many different ways to organize a case, including:

Need-Plan: Show that there is a serious, inherent problem; present a plan; show the plan will solve the problem.

Comparative Advantages: Present a plan, then show it will achieve an advantage.

Goals-Criteria Case: Show that we should strive to achieve a goal; that the present system does not achieve the goal; present a plan; show the plan will achieve the goal.

Net-Benefits: Show that the present system is achieving a net disadvantage; present a plan; show the plan will gain a net advantage.

Criteria Case (for Lincoln-Douglas and CEDA debate): Show that there is an important goal that needs to be met, then show that the value object meets that goal.

See also: CRITERIA CASE, GOALS-CRITERIA CASE, MODULAR CASE, NEED-PLAN CASE, NET BENEFITS CASE, NO-NEEDS CASE

caseside

Definition: The arguments in the debate that center on the issues directly raised by the affirmative case. In a policy debate, the affirmative advantages, including significance, inherency, and solvency, are the caseside issues. In a value debate, the affirmative's value support, including criteria and case meeting the criteria, are the caseside issues.

Usage: Go to caseside. *(In your notes of the debate, direct your attention to the issues the affirmative presented in their first speech.)* We outweigh caseside. *(Our arguments against their plan or value are more important than the affirmative's arguments and therefore we should win the debate.)*

See also: OFFCASE, PLANSIDE

caseside barrier
Definition: An inherency standard that shows that something prevents the present system from solving a problem or achieving an advantage.
Example: The current system's reliance on lawyer self-regulation prevents the solving of unethical law practices.
Usage: What is your caseside barrier? *(What argument do you make that shows the present system is not solving the problem you cite?)*
See also: INHERENCY, INHERENT BARRIER, PLANSIDE BARRIER

causal link
Definition: An argument that shows one event creates another.
Example: A new prison rebuilding program would cause a budget crisis because of its high costs.
Usage: Where's your causal link in this nuclear war disadvantage? *(Which of your arguments shows that the plan will cause nuclear war?)*
See also: ASSOCIATION, RELATIONSHIP

causality
Definition: The issue of whether a causal link exists.
Synonym: CAUSATION
See: CAUSAL LINK

causation
Definition: The issue of whether a causal link exists.
Synonym: CAUSALITY
See: CAUSAL LINK

cause and effect relationship
See: CAUSAL LINK

causes
Definition: To state that a causal link exists between two events.
See: CAUSAL LINK

certainty

Definition: Definite; confidence that something is true.

Usage: This is a certainty. *(This is definitely true.)* To a degree of certainty, I am sure. *(I am fairly confident that this is true.)*

See also: PROBABILITY

championship division

Definition: A group of the best and most experienced debate teams that compete against each other at a debate tournament.

Usage: Who is in "champ" division? *(Who is competing in the division with the best teams?)*

See also: DIVISION, TOURNAMENT

circuit

Definition: A group of debaters, coaches, and judges who regularly engage in academic debate. The "national" circuit includes debaters, coaches, and judges who are involved in academic debate at larger tournaments throughout the country. The "local" circuit would include those debaters, coaches, and judges who are involved at usually smaller tournaments in a certain region or state.

Usage: Who's going to be on the circuit? *(Who will be the debaters, coaches, and judges who will be participating in academic debate next year?)* What's the circuit like this year? *(Are the debates good this year?; or Is it a fun group to be around in debate this year?)*

See also: DIVISION

circular reasoning

See: ARGUING IN A CIRCLE

circumvention

Definition: An argument that shows a law, program, or policy is not working or will not work because of forces outside the law, program, or policy's control.

Example: Prohibition failed to stop alcohol use because it was *circumvented* by organized crime, which sold alcohol illegally. A cutoff by the United States of its arms sales to a country might fail because it could be *circumvented* by other countries selling weapons.

Usage: We argued circumvention against their plan. *(We argued that their plan would not solve a problem because forces outside of the plan's control would continue to create the problem.)*

See also: CIRCUMVENTION ARGUMENT, MECHANISM, MOTIVE, SOLVENCY

circumvention argument

Definition: A circumvention argument usually includes a mechanism to get around the law, program, or policy and a motive for doing so.

Example: A cutoff of U.S. arms sales will still allow foreign countries to sell arms (the mechanism) and many of these foreign countries want to sell arms for profits (motive).

See also: CIRCUMVENTION, MECHANISM, MOTIVE, SOLVENCY

claim

Definition: The main point of an argument; the label of an argument; the statement of what will be proven.

Example: Claim: Elections are corrupted by money.
Support: The *Buckley vs. Valeo* case showed that campaign donations were unduly influencing elections.

Usage: What is your claim? *(What is the main point of your argument?)* Have you proven this claim? *(Have you supported your argument with evidence or a good reason?)*

Synonyms: LABEL, SLUG

See also: TOULMIN MODEL OF ARGUMENT

clarify

Definition: To make an issue or argument easier to understand.

Example: Since the judge did not understand what the electromagnetic pulse blackout issue was, the debater *clarified* the argument: "If a nuclear weapon goes off, it will send off so much electricity that all communication through satellites will be impossible."

Usage: The negative needed to clarify what their position was in this round. *(The negative team needed to explain and make clear what they supported in this round.)* I will clarify my partner's answer in cross-examination. *(I will explain and make clear my debate partner's answer given in the questioning period.)*

See also: CRYSTALLIZE

clash

Definition: Directly responding to opposition arguments.

Example: The argument "Airplanes are currently very safe" *clashes* with the argument "Airplane safety has dramatically decreased."

Usage: The negative failed to clash with the affirmative case. *(The negative did not directly respond to the affirmative arguments presented in the first affirmative speech.)*

See also: COUNTERARGUMENT, FOUR-STEP REFUTATION, REBUTTAL (2), REFUTATION

classification

Definition: To apply a general argument to a specific case.

Example: Because sex education works elsewhere, it will work in this city.

Synonym: SPECIALIZATION

See also: DEDUCTION, GENERIC ARGUMENT, GENERIC DISADVANTAGE, GENERIC VALUE OBJECTION, REASONING

cliques

Definition: A group of debaters who share evidence, talk with each other, help each other, and, for the most part, interact only among themselves.

Usage: Those eastern schools are all such a bunch of cliques. *(The debaters from the East are always hanging out with each other to the exclusion of other people.)*

See also: TEAM (1)

closed minded

Definition: To be unwilling to be persuaded by arguments that one disagrees with.

Example: The judge was *closed minded:* He refused to listen to the abortion arguments simply because he disagreed with those arguments.

Usage: She's so closed minded. *(She won't listen to arguments she disagrees with.)*

See also: BIAS, INTERVENTION, TABULA RASA

coach

Definition: A person who helps students improve their debating and speaking skills. Coaches accompany their teams to tournaments, critique practicing debaters, and help organize the team.

Usage: She's the best coach. *(She, the person in charge of skills development on a team, really helps us to improve.)* He's the administrator and she's the coach. *(He organizes the team, plans trips, and handles funding for the team; she helps with skills development.)*

See also: ADMINISTRATOR OF DEBATE, DIRECTOR OF DEBATE

cogency

Definition: Arguments or positions that make sense as a whole; arguments which work together effectively.

Example: *Cogent* positions might be two negative arguments that show, first, that the present system is moving too slowly to solve a problem, and second, that the affirmative plan would cause serious new problems by acting too quickly. *Non-cogent* positions might be affirmative arguments that show free speech should be encouraged and at the same time criminals should be jailed. The two arguments don't contradict; they just don't seem to work well together.

Usage: I didn't feel the affirmative made a cogent argument for their case. *(I wasn't convinced by the affirmative arguments because I didn't see the affirmative arguments effectively working together to make a case.)*

See also: CONDITIONALITY, CONTRADICTIONS, HYPOTHESIS TESTING, INCONSISTENCY, PARADOX

commission

Definition: An appointed group of people who study and make recommendations on an issue.

Example: The Grace *Commission* studied waste in the government and suggested ways to reduce government costs. A bipartisan Central American *commission* studied Central American problems and offered suggestions for improvement. An affirmative team in a policy debate might suggest the appointment of a *commission* to examine an issue.

See also: BOARD, MANDATES, PLAN

Committee on Intercollegiate Debate and Discussion

Definition: An organization of leading representatives of the debate and discussion communities that chooses college debate propositions.

See also: NATIONAL FORENSIC LEAGUE

communication

Definition: The use of writing, gesturing, speaking, or any device of exchanging information for the purpose of persuading, educating, entertaining, conversing, or arguing between people.

Usage: The affirmative speakers failed to communicate in this round. *(The affirmative speakers failed to make their ideas clear in the debate, perhaps because they slurred their speech or because they talked too fast for the judge.)*

See also: DELIVERY, SPEAKER

comparative advantage

Definition: A type of case argument that shows a plan achieves an improvement over the present system; support for a plan that emphasizes a benefit instead of a problem.

Example: The following are examples of comparative advantage arguments: "Let's go to the beach because it would be fun"; "Affirmative action helps improve minority opportunities." An argument emphasizing the problem, such as "It's cold in here, so you should shut the door," would probably not be considered a comparative advantage. An outline of a comparative advantage:

I. Increasing farm aid would help prevent farm bankruptcies.
   A. We need more farm aid because famers can't repay their loans.
   B. Current farm aid will not help farmers enough.
   C. Increasing aid will help farmers repay loans and stop bankruptcies.

Usage: They ran a comparative advantage case. *(They argued that their plan would do better than the present system, and they did not emphasize the problem; or The affirmative argued a case that was structured like a comparative advantage case as noted previously with I, A, B, and C.)*

See also: CASE STRUCTURES

comparison

Definition: Directly noting similarities and differences between positions; weighing the advantages and disadvantages of a plan, or the support and objections of a value object.

Usage: Let's compare the status quo with the affirmative plan. *(Let's look at the differences and similarities between the present system and the affirmative plan.)*

See also: SYSTEMS ANALYSIS, WEIGH

competition (1)

Definition: A required choice between competing plans or values; the impossibility or undesirability of having the plan and the counterplan (policy debate); the impossibility or undesirability of having a value alternative and a value object (value debate).

Example: In policy debate, a negative counterplan that banned any national health insurance would be *competitive* with an affirmative plan for national health insurance. The counterplan is *competitive* because it is impossible for it to exist at the same time that the affirmative plan exists—a plan mandating health insurance and one mandating no health insurance cannot coexist. This forces the judge to choose either the plan or the counterplan. In value debate, with the topic "RESOLVED: That drug testing is bad," a *competitive* affirmative value alternative to drug testing might be employee assistance programs, provided the affirmative could show it was undesirable to drug test while having an employee assistance program.

Usage: The counterplan was not competitive. *(The plan and the counterplan could be done at the same time; therefore, the counterplan was not an argument against the plan, it was an argument to do something in addition to the plan.)*

See also: ARTIFICIAL COMPETITION, CAPTURE, MUTUAL EXCLUSIVITY, NET-BENEFITS, PERMUTATION, PHILOSOPHICAL COMPETITIVENESS, REDUNDANCY

competition (2)

Definition: The excitement of an event created by the desire to win and to do well.

Example: Delilah loved the *competition* at debate tournaments because she could try to do her very best against other opponents.

Usage: That tournament has really good competition. *(Good debate teams debate each other at that tournament.)*

See also: LOSE, WIN

competitiveness

Definition: The issue of whether a counterplan or value alternative creates a required choice; the issue of whether there is competition or not.

See also: COMPETITION (1)

concede

Definition: To admit defeat.

Example: Suyo *conceded* when she admitted, in front of the judge, that she had no chance to win the debate.

See also: FORFEIT, LOSE

concise

Definition: To clearly state an argument in the fewest words possible.

Example: A *concise* way of stating that "Cars built in America pollute very little amounts of pollutant emissions that harm the clean air in the country" might be "American cars pollute relatively little."

Usage: He was really concise in his 1AR. *(He stated his arguments in as few words as possible during his first affirmative rebuttal.)*

See also: WORD ECONOMY

conclusion

Definition: The ending comments of a case or speech.

Example: At the end of an electoral college case, a *conclusion* might be "Given the lack of true democratic representation in the electoral college, we urge you to vote affirmative and support popular-based elections."

See also: CASE, INTRODUCTION

conclusionary evidence

Definition: Support for an argument that merely repeats the claim in the same or different words; evidence that gives no reason or empirical documentation to support the claim.

Example: *Claim:* Emission control devices cause unemployment.

Conclusionary Evidence: People lose their jobs as a result of emission control devices.

Claim: Topicality is a voting issue.

Conclusionary Evidence: Topicality is a fundamental debate issue that can be voted upon.

Usage: That's conclusionary evidence. *(That evidence did not support the argument because it did not give a reason to support the argument.)*

See also: ARGUING IN A CIRCLE, BEGGING THE QUESTION

conditional

Definition: To be dependent upon the loss of another argument; inconsistent.

Example: We will argue that car dealers are not cheating customers; but if they are cheating, we will argue it is legal, and if it is not legal, we will argue that cheating is good.

Usage: This argument is conditional upon whether the value of liberty is good. *(This argument is valid if liberty is shown to be bad and irrelevant if the value is good.)*

See also: CONDITIONAL COUNTERPLAN, DISPOSITION, HYPOTHESIS TESTING, INCONSISTENCY

conditional counterplan

Definition: A negative plan that is supported by the negative if they lose or win another argument.

Example: "We will argue that there is no homeless problem; but if there is a problem, we will argue a *conditional counterplan* to have states act to help the homeless." Having the states act is conditional because it is dependent upon the team losing the argument that there are no homeless.

Usage: Drop the conditional counterplan. *(Ignore the counterplan because we will win a different argument.)* The counterplan is conditional upon the disadvantages. *(If we win the disadvantages, ignore the counterplan;* or *If we win the counterplan, ignore the disadvantages.)*

See also: CONDITIONAL, COUNTERPLAN, DISPOSITION, HYPOTHESIS TESTING

conditional counterresolution
See: CONDITIONAL COUNTERPLAN

conditionality
Definition: The issue of whether conditional arguments are legitimate.
Usage: Conditionality is illegitimate. *(Making inconsistent arguments and arguments that depend on losing other arguments is not appropriate.)*
See also: CONDITIONAL, DISPOSITION, HYPOTHESIS TESTING

conference style of debate
Definition: A type of debate in which the debaters state their positions, and then, by debating and discussing issues, seek to find the best proposal.
See also: DEBATE FORMATS

confrontation
Definition: To directly bring opposing arguments or ideas to the attention of another person.
Example: *Confrontation* might occur during the questioning period in a debate. The question "Isn't your plan going to hurt minorities?" would confront the respondent by bringing to her attention that her plan may hurt minorities.
Usage: She was really confrontational. *(She strongly brought forth her points in a rude manner.)* He confronted her about the evidence. *(He brought to her attention a flaw in the evidence.)*
See also: ARGUMENT (1), CLASH, DEBATE

Congress
Definition: The House and Senate; passes laws that go into action if the President signs them or if two-thirds or more approve of the law after the President vetoes the law.
See also: ADMINISTRATION

Congressional Digest
Definition: Reviews important bills and activities of the Congress.
See also: CONGRESSIONAL RECORD, RESEARCH

Congressional Record

Definition: A written record of congressional speeches, proposed bills, and articles requested by congressional members.

See also: CONGRESSIONAL DIGEST, RESEARCH

connotation

Definition: Infers another meaning.

Example: Saying that a plan would be protectionist might *connote* that it would create a trade war.

See also: EXTRAPOLATION, INFERENCE

consensus

Definition: Nearly unanimous agreement.

Example: There is a *consensus* among health officials that cigarettes are dangerous to people's health.

Usage: The consensus of experts is that nuclear proliferation is terrible. *(The vast majority of experts agree that the spread of nuclear weapons is terrible.)*

See also: AGREEMENT

consistency

Definition: The degree to which positions remain compatible; the degree to which arguments work together; arguments that do not contradict, but appear to support the same position.

Example: To argue that cigarettes cause little cancer is *consistent* with the argument that cigarettes should not be banned since the arguments are not contradictory and both support cigarettes.

Usage: Is it consistent to argue that space missions save money and to argue that they kill people? *(Do the arguments that space missions save money and that space missions kill people appear to support the same position?)*

See also: COGENCY, CONDITIONALITY, DISPOSITION, HYPOTHESIS TESTING, INCONSISTENCY, SYSTEMS ANALYSIS

constructive

Definition: The first speeches in a debate, in which initial positions and arguments are presented.

Example: The first four speeches in high school policy, NDT and CEDA debates and the first two speeches in a Lincoln-Douglas debate are called *constructives*.

Usage: That was a great constructive argument. *(That argument you gave in your first speech was great.)* That wasn't a very good constructive. *(That speech, given early in the debate, wasn't very good.)*

See also: REBUTTAL (1), SPEAKER ORDER

contention

Definition: A major claim; a main section of a case.

Example: The major claim "Contention One: U.S. Middle East policy increases the risk of war" would be supported by more arguments that showed how the policy increases the risk of war.

See also: OBSERVATION, OUTLINE ORGANIZATION, OVERVIEW, UNDERVIEW

contextual (standard)

Definition: A topicality standard that supports giving meaning to words by how they make sense in the resolution.

Example: On a topic "RESOLVED: That the United States should reduce its arms sales to foreign countries," a contextual standard would be to define "arms" as weapons or military items, not as appendages of the body.

Usage: Words should be defined contextually. *(The words in the topic for debate should be defined so they allow the resolution to make sense.)*

See also: FIELD EXPERT, REASONABLE STANDARD, STANDARD

contradiction

Definition: Two arguments or positions that oppose each other. One argument supports a point, while the other is against the point.

Example: To argue that there is poverty and that there is not poverty is *contradictory*. To argue for increased nuclear weapons and for getting rid of nuclear weapons is *contradictory*.

Usage: Those arguments contradict. *(One of those arguments is for something; the other is against that same thing.)*

See also: CONSISTENCY, DOUBLETURN, INCONSISTENCY

correlation

Definition: One event is considered to cause another event because the two events occur simultaneously and because other factors are not involved.

Example: A causal link, "Cigarette smoking causes cancer," is supported by the correlation, "Studies show that smokers with the same social and economic characteristics are at a greater risk of getting cancer than are nonsmokers."

Usage: This is just a correlation. *(This causal relationship is not absolutely proven; the cause may actually be something not considered.)*

See also: ALTERNATE CAUSALITY, ASSOCIATION, CAUSAL LINK, RELATIONSHIP

cost-benefit analysis

Definition: A comparison of the good and bad effects of a value or policy.

Example: If you weigh the risk of nuclear war caused by disarmament proposals versus the loss of lives due to poverty. I would urge voting against disarmament.

See also: COMPARATIVE ADVANTAGE, SYSTEMS ANALYSIS

counter

Definition: To argue against.

Example: She says that acid rain hurts trees. I will *counter* that by arguing that acid rain does not affect trees.

Usage: That runs counter to my experience. *(That argument doesn't jibe with what I know to be true.)*

See also: COUNTERARGUMENT, COUNTERPLAN, REBUTTAL, REFUTATION

counteracting causality

Definition: An unaccounted for reason that would prevent a plan, policy, or value from solving a problem.

Example: The plan to decrease acid rain by cutting pollution from coal plants won't work because car pollution will dramatically rise and increase acid rain.

See also: ALTERNATE CAUSALITY, SOLVENCY

counterargument

Definition: An argument that directly responds to an opponent's argument.

Example: The response "Cars are not dangerous" would be a *counterargument* to the argument "Cars are dangerous." A response that in some form or another said "They didn't prove cars are dangerous" is not a *counterargument,* it is a press or refutation.

See also: CLASH, COUNTER, COUNTEREXAMPLE, FOUR-STEP REFUTATION, PRESS, REFUTATION

counterclaim

Definition: A counterargument without evidence.

See: COUNTERARGUMENT

counter-criteria

Definition: The negative's criteria; an opposing standard of what must be proven to win; an opposing standard of the most important value or goal.

Example: "It is the team which can show the greatest reduction in the risk of nuclear war, not a decrease in poverty, that should win this debate."

See also: CRITERIA, GOAL, STANDARD, VALUE

counterexample

Definition: An example that is directly opposite of another.

Example: A *counterexample* of "Texas sex education programs fail" would be "Minnesota sex education programs are successful."

See also: CLASH, COUNTER, COUNTERARGUMENT

counterplan

Definition: An alternative to the affirmative plan that is advocated by the negative. A counterplan should be non-topical—against the resolution—since the negative is supposed to be against the resolution. Counterplans should be competitive—impossible or undesirable to implement with the affirmative plan—because that forces the judge to make a choice between the counterplan and plan. And, finally, counterplans should be superior to the affirmative plan.

Example: A *counterplan* against a plan for increased U.S. ties with Nicaragua on the resolution "RESOLVED: That the United States should improve its relations with a Central American country" might be that the United States should invade Nicaragua. The negative could argue that invading Nicaragua was non-topical because it does not improve relations as the topic calls for. The negative could also argue that this "invade Nicaragua" counterplan was competitive because it would be difficult to have improved relations with Nicaragua while the United States was invading the country. Then the negative could argue that their counterplan was superior because it would decrease communism.

Usage: What is your counterplan? *(What is your negative plan?)*

See also: AGENT COUNTERPLAN, ARTIFICIAL COMPETITION, CAPTURE, COMPETITIVENESS, EXCEPTIONS COUNTERPLAN, EXTRA-COMPETITIVE, MUTUAL EXCLUSIVITY, NET BENEFITS, NON-TOPICAL, PERMUTATION, PHILOSOPHICAL COMPETITIVENESS, REDUNDANCY, RESOLUTIONAL STANDARD, TOPICALITY

counterposition

Definition: A stand on an issue that directly opposes another stand.

Example: The affirmative position is for national health insurance. The negative *counterposition* is that private insurance is superior.

See also: COUNTERARGUMENT, COUNTERPLAN, PHILOSOPHY, POSITION

counterresolution

See: COUNTERPLAN

countervalue

Definition: An argument that shows a value is bad.

Example: The affirmative may argue that the value of privacy is most important; a negative *countervalue* would show that privacy is bad.

Note: Some might find this dictionary's definition of "value objection" to be a better definition of a countervalue.

See also: CRITERIA, VALUE OBJECTION

counterwarrant

Definition: In policy debate, a disadvantage that applies to a large part of the resolution but does not apply to the affirmative plan; in value debate, a value objection that applies to the value object but not to the affirmative value example.

Example: On the resolution "RESOLVED: That the United States should increase economic ties with Europe," an affirmative might present a plan that supports economic ties with Denmark. *Counterwarrants* against this affirmative might include a disadvantage against trade with England and France. On the resolution "RESOLVED: That economic austerity is justified," an affirmative might argue that a balanced budget (a value example) is good. *Counterwarrants* against this affirmative might include value objections against budget cutbacks.

See also: DISADVANTAGE, GENERIC DISADVANTAGE, HASTY GENERALIZATION, REPRESENTATIVE, TYPICALITY, VALUE EXAMPLE, VALUE OBJECT, VALUE OBJECTION

credibility

Definition: The trust an audience has in a speaker.

Example: Elliot Abrams lost *credibility* when he admitted to lying to Congress. A debater might gain *credibility* by showing her knowledge of the topic.

criteria

Definition: That which must be proven to win; the most important values, goals, or standards in a debate. Criteria generally should include a specific value, goal, or standard, a demonstration of how to meet that value, goal, or standard, and the importance of the value, goal, or standard.

Example: The *criterion* might be "The team that can show the greatest reduction in poverty will win." The full criteria might include the following:

I. The most important value is avoiding Third World nuclear proliferation.

    A. Third World proliferation presents many dangers.

    B. Slowing Third World proliferation would be beneficial.

C. Avoiding nuclear proliferation is the most important goal.

See also: COUNTER-CRITERIA, CRITERIA CASE, GOAL, STANDARD, VALUE

criteria case

Definition: A type of case used frequently in value debate that includes criteria and how the value object supports the criteria.

Example: The resolution is "RESOLVED: That legalizing drugs would be detrimental to society." A criteria case will show that the value object, legalizing drugs, does support the criteria of what is detrimental to society. Here is a criteria case:

I. (Criteria) Drug abuse should be avoided.

   A. Drug abuse kills many people.

   B. Even small increases in drug abuse would be terrible.

   C. Drug abuse is the worst threat to our society.

II. (Case) Legalizing drugs will increase drug abuse.

   A. Empirically, it has happened.

   B. Logically, it would happen.

   C. It would devastate our society.

See also: CASE STRUCTURES, CRITERIA, VALUE OBJECT

critic

See: JUDGE

critic of argument

Definition: A judge who makes a decision for the side that presented the most justified position based upon a "textual analysis" of the quality of arguments presented. The quality is determined by the judge's knowledge of what constitutes a sound argument. A critic of argument judge would not agree with every argument a debater presented just because the debater made the argument. The critic of argument would critically examine the argument to see if it was well argued. Based on the parts of the argument that are well argued, the critic would agree to that good part of the argument.

See also: PARADIGM, TABULA RASA

cross-apply

Definition: The use of an argument made on a different issue.

Usage: On their argument showing that coal plants would actually increase nuclear waste, please cross-apply the B-2 point, which showed there will be less nuclear waste because coal plants will replace nuclear plants. *(Our previous argument, which showed there would be less nuclear waste because coal plants would replace nuclear plants, proves that their argument showing increased nuclear waste is false.)*

See also: CLASH, COUNTER

cross-examination

Definition: The questioning period in a debate. After each speaker finishes his or her constructive speech, that speaker responds to questions by one of his or her opponents during cross-examination.

Usage: That cross-ex was really good. *(That questioning period was really good.)* Remember her cross-examination answer when she said the affirmative plan would cut tree imports. *(Remember that when asked during the questioning period, she said the affirmative plan would cut tree imports.)*

See also: ANSWER, QUESTION, RESPONDENT, RESPONSE

Cross-Examination Debate Association

See: CEDA

crystallize

Definition: To clarify a series of arguments and to explain why those arguments mean one should win the debate; to synthesize.

Example: A debater *crystallizing* the issues might argue, "So, what we have shown you is that business should not be taxed because that would cause a loss of jobs and perhaps even lead to a severe recession. You should vote against their plan because the economic losses outweigh whatever little environmental benefits they will gain."

See also: SYNTHESIS

D

data

See: EVIDENCE

debatability

Definition: The issue of whether an interpretation of an issue allows it to be debated. If Team X argues that any opposing argument made would actually be an argument for Team X, the issue would not be debatable.

Example: If on the topic "RESOLVED: That drug interdiction is the best way to stop drugs from entering the United States" an affirmative said that "drug interdiction" was *any* effort to stop drugs, the negative could never show that anything was better to stop drugs than drug interdiction. By definition, anything that stopped drugs would be drug interdiction and would therefore be an affirmative argument. This interpretation would make the resolution not *debatable*.

Usage: Debatability should be the standard for evaluating topicality. *(The interpretation of the resolution should allow both sides to make good arguments.)*

See also: BIDIRECTIONALITY, TOPICALITY

debate

Definition: A disagreement in which two sides take opposing positions on an issue and attempt to convince a judge or an audience that their position is superior to the other.

Example: The Bush–Dukakis *debates* are good examples of audience *debates.* When a brother and sister argue over who broke the television set in order to convince their mom, they are *debating.* When one team argues for the death penalty and the other against in order to convince their judge to vote for them, there is a *debate.*

See also: ARGUMENT (2), DEBATE FORMATS, DISPUTE

debate formats

Definition: Types of debate that differ in their goals, rules, and practices.

See also: ARGUMENT BY ARGUMENT DEBATE, BRITISH FORMAT DEBATE, CEDA DEBATE, CONFERENCE STYLE, DIRECT CLASH DEBATE, HIGH SCHOOL DEBATE, LINCOLN-DOUGLAS DEBATE, MICHIGAN STYLE, MONTANA STYLE, NDT DEBATE, OFF-TOPIC DEBATE, OREGON STYLE, OXFORD STYLE, POLICY DEBATE, PORTLAND STYLE, SHIFT OF OPINION DEBATE, WASHINGTON STYLE

decision

Definition: The statement of which side in the debate won the debate.

Example: "I voted for the negative team because they showed that election practices are helping democracy by giving access to third parties."

Usage: What was the decision? *(Did the judges vote for the affirmative or the negative?)* That wasn't a very good decision. *(The judge didn't give a good reason to vote for the side he or she did.)*

See also: JUDGE, REASON FOR DECISION

decision rule

Definition: A standard for choosing which side to vote for.

Usage: This is a decision rule. Third World poverty must be reduced. *(The team that most decreases Third World poverty should win the debate.)*

See also: STANDARD

deduction

Definition: To reason that a general rule applies to a specific example.

Example: Because Toyotas do not work, this Toyota won't. Since drug education programs usually fail, the ones at our school will, too.

Antonym: INDUCTION

See also: CLASSIFICATION, EXTRAPOLATION, GENERALIZATION, INFERENCE, REASONING

defense

Definition: The support of a position in response to attacks.

Example: "They attacked our argument which said blacks are discriminated against. I must disagree. First . . . ."

Usage: They were on the defense that round. *(They responded to opponent attacks but did not rebuild their own case and hence seemed to be in a weaker position.)*

See also: PRESS, REBUTTAL (2), REFUTATION

defense of the status quo

Definition: Support for the present system against a proposed change.

Example: A negative *defending the status quo* might argue, "The negative will defend the status quo in this round by supporting the current Superfund environmental cleanup. Doing any more than the Superfund, like the affirmative plan, would cost too much."

See also: COUNTERPLAN, MINOR REPAIR, NEGATIVE

definition

Definition: The description of a word or phrase's meaning.

Example: A *definition* of the phrase "free speech" in a resolution "RESOLVED: That free speech ought to be considered an absolute value" might be "people speaking as in talking," or it could be broader: "any spoken, written, filmed, or otherwise communicated message."

Usage: What is your definition standard? *(According to your arguments, what would make a good definition?)*

See also: BEST DEFINITION, REASONABLE STANDARD, STANDARD, TOPICALITY

delivery

Definition: The presentation of a speech, including eye contact, vocal variety, gestures, poise, and appearance.

Usage: She had good delivery. *(She presented her speech well.)*

See also: COMMUNICATION, SPEAKER, STYLE

Delta Sigma Rho–Tau Kappa Alpha (DSR–TKA)

Definition: A college speech and debate organization.

See also: PI KAPPA DELTA, SPEAKER AND GAVEL

denial

Definition: To disagree that one has said or done something; to disagree that the opponent's arguments are valid.

Example: We *deny* that the present system is leaving people without shelter.

See also: PRESS, REFUTATION

description

Definition: To give the defining characteristics of something, especially a policy or value.

Example: "The present system includes a program that gives loans and some subsidies but does not give any aid."

See also: COMPARISON, SYSTEMS ANALYSIS

desirability

Definition: Whether an event is wanted or not.

Example: Teams might debate the *desirability* of saving lives of animals by arguing whether saving animal lives is good or bad.

Usage: What is the desirability of further pollution control devices? *(How much do we really want further pollution control devices?)*

See also: ADVANTAGE, BENEFIT

develop

Definition: To add support for a position by bolstering it with supporting arguments.

Example: To *develop* an argument "Animals are mistreated in labs," one might add supporting arguments like "Lab animals are mutilated," "Baby animals in the labs are taken from their mothers," and "Lab animals are inadequately fed."

See also: ANALYSIS

devil terms
Definition: Words or phrases with negative connotations.
Example: communism, child abuse, arms race, fascism
Antonym: GOD TERMS

Dewey Decimal system
Definition: Books in a library are sometimes organized into the Dewey Decimal system. The books are ordered numerically and alphabetically with call numbers like "619.9 BD."
See also: LIBRARY OF CONGRESS

dialectic
Definition: The comparison of differing arguments to search for the best ideas and actions.
See also: LOGIC, RHETORIC, SOPHISTRY

dilemma
Definition: A dilemma occurs when a debater's position must lead to one of two or more bad conclusions.
Example: Funding new social spending places one in the *dilemma* of choosing between cutting other programs, deficit spending, or increasing taxes.
See also: CONDITIONALITY, CONSISTENCY, CONTRADICTION, DOUBLETURN, INCONSISTENCY

direct clash debate
Definition: A type of debate in which the debaters respond directly to their opponent's arguments.
Example: If one debater argues that we should cut off aid to South Africa, his opponent is likely to argue that aid should not be cut off, and to directly attack each of his arguments.
See also: DEBATE FORMATS

direct refutation
See: CLASH

director of debate/forensics
Definition: The director of forensics is usually a professor at a college or university who helps set up and manage team activities. The director of forensics may or may not coach the team.
See also: ADMINISTRATOR OF DEBATE, COACH, TEAM

disadvantage

Definition: A reason against taking a course of action; to show a plan will cause a harm. Usually includes links and impacts, and sometimes brinks.

Example: A *disadvantage* against a plan for increased prison sentencing of criminals might be:
I. Increased prison sentencing would cause a jail nightmare.
   A. (Links) Prison sentencing would increase overcrowding.
   B. (Impacts) Overcrowding would cause jail rioting.

Usage: Where's the growth disadvantage? *(Where is the written argument showing that economic growth is bad?)* That is disadvantageous. *(That would cause serious harms.)*

See also: ADVANTAGE, BRINK, IMPACT, LINKS, TURNAROUND, UNIQUENESS, VALUE OBJECTION

disco

Definition: To drop or agree with certain arguments in a debate in order to make a case for winning the debate.

Example: The affirmative knew that the part of their plan that called for increased taxes caused a huge disadvantage, so, in the first affirmative rebuttal, they stated that they no longer supported the tax because the negative had shown the tax was not topical. So the affirmative supported only the no-cost part of their plan, workfare, and they were clearly winning that part of their plan. This dropping out of the taxes and supporting just the workfare in order to win would be a *disco.*

Usage: That disco was not fair. *(That dropping of certain arguments to win was not fair, probably because it did not allow the other team a chance to respond, it misrepresented the arguments, or it dropped arguments that could not be dropped.)*

See also: ALTERNATIVE JUSTIFICATION CASE, CONDITIONALITY, GAMESPLAYER, HYPOTHESIS TESTING, SEVER

discretionary powers

Definition: The powers available to a board administering a policy or plan.

Example: The board overseeing an affirmative plan seeking to stop Contra aid might be given *discretionary power* to inspect and review government documents.
See also: ADMINISTRATION, BOARD, PLAN, POLICY

discussion
Definition: The use of arguments among people to come to an agreement to take an action or to agree with some belief.
Example: A small group might have *discussion* on whether medical experiments using animals are immoral. The group members would make arguments on all sides of the animal rights issue and seek to come to some kind of agreement on whether experimentation involving animals is immoral.
See also: ARGUMENT (1), DEBATE, DISPUTE

dismiss
Definition: To respond to an argument by rejecting its importance.
Example: Instead of spending time on the argument showing the plan would hurt military preparedness, the debater *dismissed* it quickly by arguing that the military would not be affected.
Usage: Dismiss that argument they made about the nuclear war. *(Quickly answer their nuclear war argument by showing it is unimportant.)*
See also: REFUTATION

disposition
Definition: To describe how one's conditional arguments are consistent with each other.
Example: If there is a serious drug abuse problem, then you should vote for the conditional counterplan to drug test people. If there isn't a serious drug abuse problem, then you should vote for the conditional counterplan to legalize drugs.
See also: CONDITIONAL COUNTERPLAN, CONDITIONALITY, CONSISTENCY, CONTRADICTION, HYPOTHESIS TESTING

dispute
Definition: A debate without a specified judge.
Example: Two neighbors might have a *dispute* about whether one of their homes is too close to the property line.
See also: DEBATE, DISCUSSION

distortion
See: MISREPRESENT

diversionary proofs

Definition: To make arguments that appear to respond to an opponent's argument but actually do not directly respond to the argument.

Example: "They claim that the Japanese trade deficit is high. Well, Japanese products are good." This is a *diversionary proof* because, while it may appear that arguing Japanese products are good will respond to the Japanese trade deficit issue, it does not directly show that the Japanese trade deficit is not high and hence is diverting the issue.

See also: FALLACY, PERIPHERAL ARGUMENT, RED HERRING, STRAWPERSON FALLACY

division

Definition: A group of debate teams that debate each other at a debate tournament. Teams in different divisions do not debate each other.

Usage: What division are you in? *(What group of debaters do you debate?)*

See also: CHAMPIONSHIP DIVISION, EXPERIENCED DIVISION, INEXPERIENCED DIVISION, INTERMEDIATE DIVISION, JUNIOR DIVISION, NOVICE DIVISION, OPEN DIVISION, SENIOR DIVISION

division of labor

Definition: The separate duties that each debater should fulfill in a debate. Traditionally, the division of labor is to have the first negative respond to the affirmative case arguments, while the second negative makes arguments against the affirmative plan or value example. The first negative rebuttalist does not cover the same issues argued by the second negative constructive.

Usage: You didn't follow good division of labor. *(You two debaters didn't have separate duties and wound up repeating each other's arguments or missing your opponent's arguments.)*

See also: SPEAKER DUTIES

documentation
See: EVIDENCE

documents
See: GOVERNMENT DOCUMENTS

doubleturn
Definition: To argue that what you support will cause an event that will cause another event that shows what you support is bad.
Example: Our plan will actually decrease nuclear proliferation, and nuclear proliferation is good.
See also: CONTRADICTION, TURNAROUND, TURNING THE TABLES

doubt
Definition: To be skeptical about an argument.
Usage: I doubt that is true. *(I am skeptical about that; I don't really think that is true.)* The odds of that disadvantage happening are doubtful. *(It is unlikely that the disadvantage would happen.)*
See also: CERTAINTY, PLAUSIBILITY, PROBABILITY

downtime
See: PREPARATION TIME

drop
Definition: To not respond to an argument.
Usage: He dropped that argument. *(He did not respond to that argument.)* We will drop that argument. *(We will no longer argue that point.)*
See also: BURDEN OF REBUTTAL, BURDEN OF REJOINDER, CLASH, IGNORE (AN ISSUE), PULL

E

edit

Definition: To change parts of a speech, case, or evidence.
See also: CASE CONSTRUCTION, RESEARCH

education

Definition: To increase one's understanding of the world.
Usage: Debate is an educational activity. *(Debate gives people a better understanding of their world and how to be effective in that world.)*
See also: DEBATABILITY

effects-topicality

Definition: To argue that the affirmative plan is topical because it will cause something to happen which supports the topic. The plan itself, not what it causes, must support the topic.
Example: An argument that said a plan to increase Third World trade supports the resolution "RESOLVED: That the United States should cut its arms sales" because increasing commercial trade would lead to a decrease in arms sales is probably *effects-topical.* To increase trade is not to cut arms sales. To say increased trade will have the effect of cutting arms sales makes the topic meaningless, because nearly any plan could ultimately affect arms sales.
See also: EXTRA-TOPICALITY, JUSTIFICATION, TOPICALITY

either-or argument

Definition: One of two arguments is valid; either this argument is true or that one is.

Usage: *Either* the plan increases the use of cement *or* it increases the use of asphalt to build more freeways.

See also: DILEMMA, IF-THEN ARGUMENT

elimination rounds

Definition: Final rounds where the teams with the best records in a tournament compete against each other. The loser is out; the winner advances for further competition. Usually three judges watch these rounds. Tournaments usually hold *elimination rounds* after four to eight debates. Triple-octas have sixty-four teams, double-octas have thirty-two teams, octas have sixteen teams, quarters have eight teams, semis have four teams, finals have two teams. The winner of finals takes first place. At NFL tournaments, the few teams remaining that have less than two losses are in *elimination rounds.*

Usage: Did you make it to elims? *(Did you have a good enough record to make the eliminations, the final rounds?)*

Synonyms: ELIMS, FINAL ROUNDS, OUT ROUNDS

See also: DROP, IN, LOSE, OUT, TURKEY, WIN

elims

See: ELIMINATION ROUNDS

Emory switch

Definition: Occurs when the first negative speaker attacks the affirmative plan or value example and leaves attacks against the affirmative case to the second negative speaker.

Usage: The Emory is illegitimate. *(Having the first negative attack the plan and the second negative attack the case is not appropriate.)*

See also: INSIDE-OUTSIDE

empirical

Definition: Proven by experience.

Example: The St. Paul study that examined a sex education program is an *empirical* study because the sex education program had been tested by examining how well the program had worked.

Usage: Do you have an empirical study to prove that your plan will work? *(Do you have a study that examined your plan in action where it was effective?)*

See also: EVIDENCE

enforcement

Definition: To mandate observance of the present policy or a plan.

Example: An *enforcement* plank (a part of) an affirmative plan to reduce toxic waste might state that anyone caught illegally dumping toxic waste would be fined or imprisoned.

Usage: What is your enforcement? *(How do you make sure that people will observe your plan?)*

See also: CIRCUMVENTION, PLAN, PLANK

English format debate

See: BRITISH FORMAT DEBATE

enthymeme

Definition: (1) A syllogism (since premise $a = b$, and premise $b = c$, then conclusion $a = c$) made by a speaker to appeal to an audience; (2) a syllogism with a missing premise or conclusion.

Example: (1) In front of an audience, a speaker makes this *enthymeme*. "Since severely polluting things should be banned (premise), and since diesel cars create severe pollution (premise), then diesel cars should be banned (conclusion)." In intellectual gatherings where this could be immediately tested among all the participants, it would be a syllogism. (2) "If diesel cars create severe pollution, then diesel cars should be banned" might be considered an *enthymeme* because it is missing the premise that severely polluting things should be banned.

See also: DIALECTIC, REASONING, SOPHISTRY, SYLLOGISM, TOULMIN MODEL OF ARGUMENT

escalation

Definition: A dramatic increase; a buildup of tensions or violence.

Usage: This will escalate to all-out war with the Soviet Union. *(This will lead to a buildup of violence until there is war with the Soviet Union.)*

See also: DISADVANTAGE, VALUE OBJECTION

ethical

Definition: The scholarliness, morality, and legality of someone's actions. Debaters who are courteous and use good research practices are considered *ethical*.

Usage: It is unethical to fabricate evidence. *(It is unscholarly, immoral, and illegal—according to NFL, NDT, and CEDA rules—to make up evidence.)*

See also: AGGRESSIVE

ethics

Definition: The practice or study of being ethical.

See also: ETHICAL

ethos

See: CREDIBILITY

evaluate

Definition: To carefully examine something to determine its worth.

Usage: Let's evaluate this argument that supports the deterrent effect of nuclear weapons. *(Let's examine more carefully how well nuclear weapons actually prevent war.)*

See also: ANALYSIS, COMPARISON, CRYSTALLIZE, DESCRIPTION, SYNTHESIS

evaluative claims

See: RESOLUTION OF VALUE

evidence

Definition: (1) The support for an argument, usually a quotation from a published article or book; (2) the reason why an argument is valid.

Example: (1) *Claim:* Drug tests on law enforcement applicants are constitutional.
Evidence:

> Jeffrey Higginbotham, (Special Agent, FBI Academy), FBI law enforcement bulletin, November 1986, p. 26.
> "The few court cases where this issue has arisen have uniformly concluded that drug testing of law enforcement applicants through urinalysis is lawful."

(2) *Claim:* Drug tests do not violate privacy...
Evidence: (because) everyone has medical tests and job tests that are part of one's public not private obligations.

Usage: You have no evidence to support that point. *(You have no support for that argument.)*

Synonyms: DATA, DOCUMENTATION

See also: ARGUMENT CARD, CLAIM, TOULMIN MODEL OF ARGUMENT, WARRANT

exaggeration

Definition: To overclaim; overstate a point.

Example: The argument "Our plan will solve all of the world's problems" is very probably an *exaggeration.*

Usage: "Isn't that a bit of an exaggeration? *(Aren't you overclaiming that point a bit?)*

example

Definition: One instance of a person, place, event, or thing.

Example: An *example* of drug abuse might be John Belushi's abuse of drugs. An *example* of a policy to make people who receive welfare assistance work might be the program used in Massachusetts.

Usage: Can you give me one example of the use of nuclear bombs? *(Can you give me one instance where nuclear bombs have been used?)*

See also: EMPIRICAL, HASTY GENERALIZATION, INDUCTION, REPRESENTATIVE, TYPICALITY

exceptions counterplan

Definition: A counterplan that enacts the affirmative plan minus a portion of that plan.

Example: An *exceptions counterplan* against a plan to give compensation to all brown lung victims of cotton dust might be to give compensation to all brown lung victims except those who smoke.

See also: COUNTERPLAN

existential inherency

Definition: An argument that the present system will not solve the problem or will not achieve the advantage because the problem will continue to exist or the advantage will continue to not be achieved; a view of inherency that places the burden upon the negative to prove that the present system will achieve the advantage or solve the problem.

Example: A policy affirmative case that argued only "Unemployment is high, and our plan will give jobs to everyone" is a case with *existential inherency* because it does not discuss why the present system is unable to provide jobs to everyone.

See also: COMPARATIVE ADVANTAGE, GAP INHERENCY, INHERENCY, SYSTEMS ANALYSIS

experienced division

Definition: A separate group of debate teams with experience who compete against each other.

See also: DIVISION, TOURNAMENT

expert

Definition: A person who is knowledgeable about a subject.

Example: Henry Kissinger is an *expert* on foreign affairs. A computer science professor would be an *expert* on computers.

See also: AUTHORITY, SOURCE

explicit

Definition: State openly; to make something clear by saying it.

Example: Telly makes her organization explicit when she says, "My first point will be...."

Usage: Make your organization explicit. *(Make your organization clearer by numbering or lettering your arguments, like "First...and*

second. ...") The affirmative failed to make their plan explicitly clear to me in this debate. *(The affirmative didn't state exactly what their plan would do, what action it would take.)*

Antonym: IMPLICIT
See also: CLARIFY, COMMUNICATION

extemporaneous (1)

Definition: To deliver a speech that is prepared with information gathered at any time before the speech and organized shortly before the speech. Except for the first affirmative, nearly all of the speeches in a debate are extemporaneous because while the debaters have prepared arguments long before the debate, the organization of those arguments takes place shortly before the debaters speak.

See also: DELIVERY, IMPROMPTU (1)

extemporaneous (2)

Definition: A speech event in which a speaker answers one of three questions about a politically, socially, or economically significant issue, after taking at most thirty minutes to organize prepared materials. At tournaments, students compete in extemporaneous speaking. A student might choose between topics like: "Will Gorbachev really reform the Soviet Union?," "Will the President's stand on drugs be popular?," or "Is television turning politics into pandering instead of discussing?" The student picks one of these three topic questions, prepares for thirty minutes, and then answers the question in his or her speech.

See also: IMPROMPTU (2)

extend

Definition: To rebuild a previous argument by adding fresh analysis and arguments to support that previous argument.

Example: A debater would *extend* the argument "Our trade imbalance hurts our economy" by arguing "The trade imbalance increases inflation, hurts employment, and hurts other economic growth."

See also: PULL, REBUTTAL (2)

extension

Definition: An argument or arguments that extend a previous argument.

See: EXTEND

extra-competitiveness

Definition: The issue of whether part of a counterplan or value alternative is possible and desirable to implement with the plan.

Example: The plan is to increase funds for college education. A counterplan may ban federal funds used for college education and also support increased funds for high school education. It is impossible to increase funds and ban funds for college education at the same time, so that portion of the counterplan is competitive. But it would be very easy to increase funds for high school as well as for college education. So, unless the negative could show that doing both would be undesirable for some reason, then that portion of the counterplan is *extra-competitive* and any advantages stemming from that portion of the counterplan should not be considered in a decision.

See also: ARTIFICIAL COMPETITION, CAPTURE, COMPETITIVENESS, COUNTERPLAN, EXTRA-TOPICALITY, MUTUAL EXCLUSIVITY, NET BENEFITS, PERMUTATION, REDUNDANCY, RESOLUTIONAL STANDARD

extra-topicality

Definition: The issue of whether part of a plan, counterplan, or value example does or does not support the resolution.

Example: An affirmative plan to both increase solar power and to increase nuclear power plants on the resolution "RESOLVED: That the United States should increase development of solar power" is probably *extra-topical*. The part of the plan that increases solar power stations is probably topical. The part of the plan that increases nuclear power plants does not support increased solar power development and hence is *extra-topical;* any advantages stemming from nuclear power plants should not be considered in a decision.

See also: COUNTERPLAN, EFFECTS-TOPICALITY, JUSTIFICATION, PLAN, TOPICALITY, VALUE EXAMPLE

extrapolation

Definition: To make an inference; to make a conclusion based on something that is known.

Example: Since sex education worked in St. Paul and Pomona, we might *extrapolate* and conclude that it will work throughout the country.

See also: GENERALIZATION, INFERENCE, REASONING

eye contact

Definition: To look at someone, especially when a speaker looks at an audience or judge.

Usage: John, you have bad eye contact. *(John, you don't look at the judge or audience listening to you very much; or John you look awkward when you look at your judge or audience.)*

See also: COMMUNICATION, DELIVERY, SPEAKER

F

fabrication

Definition: To make up a piece of evidence; to falsify a piece of evidence. Fabrication is considered a serious ethical breach.

Usage: Fabrication of evidence will lead to an automatic loss. *(Making up evidence will lead to a loss for the team who used the made-up evidence.)*

See also: ETHICS, EVIDENCE, RESEARCH

fact

Definition: An objective statement; a piece of information.

Example: "The United States has $1 billion in trade with China" is a *fact.* To argue "U.S. trade with China is good" is not a *fact;* it is an opinion.

See also: BELIEF, EVIDENCE, OPINION, RESOLUTION OF FACT, RESOLUTION OF VALUE

fallacy

Definition: Faulty reasoning that makes an argument weak.

Example: "We should go to the store because we should" is a *fallacy* of begging the question. "You shouldn't vote for our opponents because they are ugly" is a *fallacy* of ad hominem (attacks on people instead of on their arguments).

Usage: That is a fallacious argument. *(That is a weak argument because its reasoning is faulty.)*

See also: AD HOMINEM ATTACK, ARGUING IN A CIRCLE, BAND-WAGON FALLACY, BEGGING THE QUESTION, CONCLU-SIONARY EVIDENCE, DIVERSIONARY PROOF, NON SEQUITUR, POST HOC FALLACY, QUESTION BEGGING, SHOULD-COULD FALLACY, SHOULD-WOULD FALLACY

feasibility

Definition: The ability to do something given the constraints of a situation.

Example: It is *unfeasible* to have a world government because not all nations would agree with it and the changeover would be very difficult.

See also: SOLVENCY, WORKABILITY

feedback

Definition: A judge's or audience's response to the debater(s).

Example: The judge gave *feedback,* including smiles and several approving nods, that indicated the debater was making good arguments. After the debate, the judge gave *feedback* by telling the debaters how they could improve.

See also: JUDGE, ORAL CRITIQUE

fiat

Definition: The power of the affirmative or negative to implement their plan or counterplan; the assumption that the plan or counterplan will go into action. If the affirmative supports a plan that would take over banks, the negative cannot argue that the plan is unconstitutional and unimplementable. If the affirmative wants, it can change the Constitution and *fiat* the plan into action. (In such a case, the affirmative probably does need to say in its plan that it will change the Constitution.)

Usage: We have fiat power. *(We have the ability to pass our plan or counterplan into law.)*

See also: COUNTERPLAN, FIAT ABUSE, PLAN, SHOULD-WOULD FALLACY

fiat abuse

Definition: Occurs when the affirmative or negative claims it will stop disadvantages or circumvention arguments by its power to enact a plan or counterplan, or when there is no existing way to implement the plan or counterplan.

Example: If the negative argued people would angrily react to a take-over of banks, the affirmative would be committing *fiat abuse* if they argued that their fiat power to enact the plan made the angry people irrelevant. If the negative presented a counterplan to enact world government, they would be committing *fiat abuse* if they did not show how it could be implemented. If the negative presented a counterplan to have all fifty states do what the affirmative plan did (to gain states rights advantages), they would probably be committing *fiat abuse* since there is no mechanism that would get all fifty states to enact the same basic law at the same time.

See also: FIAT, SHOULD-WOULD FALLACY

field (1)
See: ARGUMENT FIELD

field (2)
Definition: A discipline.
Example: Physics, mathematics, political science.
See also: EXPERT

field dependence
Definition: An argument's acceptance is dependent upon the community in which it is being discussed.
Example: The argument "Criminal X is guilty" is *field dependent* because it would be more easily accepted among a group of police officers than among a group of legal scholars.
Antonym: FIELD INDEPENDENCE
See also: ARGUMENT FIELD, TOULMIN MODEL OF ARGUMENT

field expert
Definition: An authority in a discipline; a topicality standard that requires an authority in a discipline to define terms.
Example: Use the *field expert* standard because meanings of words are best known to those who use them consistently.
See also: STANDARD, TOPICALITY

field independence

Definition: An argument's acceptance is not dependent upon the community in which it is being discussed.

Example: The argument "That door is red" is *field independent* because it would be accepted with the same proof among legal scholars, police, or any group.

Antonym: FIELD DEPENDENCE

See also: ARGUMENT FIELD, FORMAL LOGIC, TOULMIN MODEL OF ARGUMENT

figurative analogy

Definition: A comparison between two unalike events or objects.

Example: "Taking an overly long bath is comparable to a grape sitting out in the sun."

See also: ANALOGY, LITERAL ANALOGY

file

Definition: An organized collection of evidence on cards or briefs.

See also: BRIEF, CARD, EVIDENCE, FILEBOX

filebox

Definition: The container holding a team's files. A plastic box or ox box that holds manilla folders is used for briefs. A metal boxtray or recipe box is used for cards.

See also: BRIEF, CARD, EVIDENCE, FILE

final rounds

See: ELIMINATION ROUNDS

first affirmative constructive

Definition: The speech in which the affirmative presents their initial reasons for supporting the resolution; the first speech in a debate. Included in a first affirmative constructive in a policy debate might be: introduction, the resolution, definitions, a plan, the plan's advantage (including significance, inherency, solvency), and a conclusion. Included in a first affirmative constructive in a value debate might be: introduction, the resolution, definitions, a criteria, a case supporting the criteria, and a conclusion.

Synonym: FIRST AFFIRMATIVE

See also: DIVISION OF LABOR, FIRST AFFIRMATIVE REBUTTAL, FIRST AFFIRMATIVE SPEAKER, SPEAKER DUTIES

first affirmative rebuttal (1)

Definition: In team debate, the speech in which the affirmative team answers the second negative constructive and first negative rebuttal arguments; the speech immediately following the first negative rebuttal. Included in a typical first affirmative rebuttal is a quick introduction, responses to the second negative planside or offcase arguments, rebuilding of the affirmative case by answering the first negative rebuttal arguments, and then a conclusion.

See also: DIVISION OF LABOR, FIRST AFFIRMATIVE CONSTRUCTIVE, FIRST AFFIRMATIVE REBUTTAL (2), FIRST AFFIRMATIVE SPEAKER, SPEAKER DUTIES

first affirmative rebuttal (2)

Definition: In Lincoln-Douglas debate, the speech in which the affirmative speaker presents responses to the first negative constructive; the speech immediately following the cross-examination of the negative speaker. Included in a typical first affirmative rebuttal in Lincoln-Douglas debate is an introduction, responses to the negative offcase arguments and a rebuilding of the affirmative case by answering the negative case arguments, and then a conclusion.

See also: EMORY SWITCH, FIRST AFFIRMATIVE CONSTRUCTIVE, FIRST AFFIRMATIVE REBUTTAL (1), FIRST AFFIRMATIVE SPEAKER, SPEAKER DUTIES

first affirmative speaker

Definition: The speaker who gives the first affirmative speech and usually the first affirmative rebuttal.

Synonym: FIRST AFFIRMATIVE

See also: DIVISION OF LABOR, EMORY SWITCH, FIRST AFFIRMATIVE CONSTRUCTIVE, FIRST AFFIRMATIVE REBUTTAL (1), FIRST AFFIRMATIVE REBUTTAL (2), SPEAKER DUTIES

first negative constructive

Definition: The speech in which the negative presents its first arguments against the affirmative; the speech immediately following the cross-examination of the first affirmative speaker. The typical first negative constructive includes a quick introduction, an observation like a topicality argument, responses to the affirmative case, then a conclusion. In a Lincoln-Douglas debate, the negative speaker will offer an offcase argument as well.

See also: DIVISION OF LABOR, FIRST NEGATIVE REBUTTAL, FIRST NEGATIVE SPEAKER, SPEAKER DUTIES

first negative rebuttal

Definition: The speech in which the negative further develops their arguments made directly against the affirmative case; the speech immediately following cross-examination of the second negative speaker (in team debate); the speech immediately following the first affirmative rebuttal (in Lincoln-Douglas debate). The first negative rebuttal typically includes an introduction, rebuilding of any observations made in the first negative constructive and of responses made against the affirmative case, and then a conclusion. In Lincoln-Douglas, the first negative rebuttal (or the negative rebuttal, as it is sometimes called), also rebuilds the offcase arguments in light of the affirmative responses.

See also: DIVISION OF LABOR, FIRST NEGATIVE CONSTRUCTIVE, FIRST NEGATIVE SPEAKER, SPEAKER DUTIES

first negative speaker

Definition: The speaker who gives the first negative constructive and first negative rebuttal speeches.
Synonym: FIRST NEGATIVE
See also: DIVISION OF LABOR, FIRST NEGATIVE CONSTRUCTIVE, FIRST NEGATIVE REBUTTAL, SPEAKER DUTIES

flexible
See: INCREMENTAL

flip
See: TURNAROUND

flip-flop

See: INSIDE-OUTSIDE

flow (1)

Definition: (*n.*) A sheet or sheets of paper which have notes of the arguments of a debate.

Example: A typical *flow* looks like this:

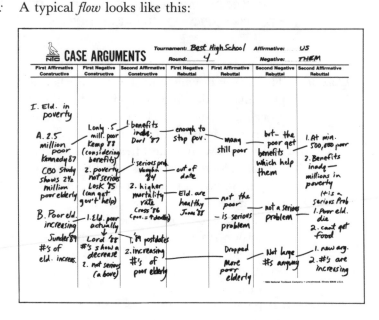

Usage: Let me see your flow. *(Let me see your notes of the arguments made in the debate.)*

See also: FLOW (2), FLOWSHEET, NOTES

flow (2)

Definition: (*v.*) To take notes of the arguments made in a debate. A judge would flow by writing down the main point of each of the debater's arguments and placing them in order so that it is clear which arguments respond to which.

Usage: Can you flow? *(Are you able to set up a proper flowsheet, take good notes of the arguments, and show which arguments responded to which?)* Start flowing. *(Start taking notes of the arguments in the debate.)*

See also: FLOW (1), NOTES

flow across

See: PULL

flowchart

See: FLOWSHEET

flowsheet

Definition: A sheet or sheets of paper that are set up to take notes of the arguments made in a debate.

Example:

🕊️ **CASE ARGUMENTS** Tournament:_____ Round:_____				Affirmative:_____ Negative:_____		
First Affirmative Constructive	First Negative Constructive	Second Affirmative Constructive	First Negative Rebuttal	First Affirmative Rebuttal	Second Negative Rebuttal	Second Affirmative Rebuttal

Synonym: FLOWCHART

See also: FLOW (1), FLOW (2), NOTES

fluency

Definition: The clarity and smoothness of one's use of language.

Usage: You need to be more fluent. *(You need to speak more smoothly, without pauses, breaks, and cracks in delivering your arguments.)*

See also: DELIVERY, SPEAKER, STYLE

Forensic

Definition: Publication of the speech and debate organization Pi Kappa Delta, emphasizing articles on speech and debate theory and practicum.

See also: SPEAKER AND GAVEL

Forensic Quarterly
Definition: A high school publication that includes articles on speech and debate, and especially analysis of the high school policy resolution.
See also: ROSTRUM

forensics
Definition: The academic activity of giving speeches and debating; speaking and arguing about legal issues.
See also: DEBATE, INDIVIDUAL EVENTS, SPEAKING

forfeit
Definition: To lose a debate round by not debating.
Example: A debater might get sick and not debate, forcing her team to *forfeit* a debate round.
See also: BYE, LOSS, NO SHOW

formal logic
Definition: The use of standardized reasoning processes; an approach to argument that assumes field independence. Syllogisms $(a = b)$ are a standard form of argument in formal logic. A premise of formal logic states that an argument is just as valid in front of one group as another.
See also: FIELD INDEPENDENCE, INFORMAL LOGIC, SYLLOGISMS

format
See: DEBATE FORMATS, SPEAKER ORDER

four-person team
Definition: A debate team which has two people debating affirmative, and two different people debating negative.
See also: THREE-PERSON TEAM

four-step refutation
Definition: A four-step process of responding to opponent arguments. First, state your opponent's argument. Second, state your argument. Third, support your argument with evidence or analysis. Fourth, impact your argument.
Example: (1) "My opponent argued that pornography is not dangerous."

(2) "First, their evidence is biased."

(3) "The source is the publisher of Penthouse."

(4) "His analysis is tainted by his desire for his magazine's profits."

(2) "Second, I will argue that pornography is dangerous to women."

(3) "According to . . .(read evidence)."

(4) "So, pornography endangers women because it exploits them and makes men more likely to commit violent acts against them."

Note: As is typical, steps 2, 3, and 4 are repeated during the four-step refutation process.

See also: CLASH, ON, REBUTTAL, REFUTATION.

future inherency

See: PERMANENCE

G

gamesplayer

Definition: A person that considers debate to be like a game. A gamesplayer judge will let a team make any argument, including "Nuclear war is good" and "Democracy is bad." A gamesplayer makes decisions on the basis of the arguments presented by the debaters, especially the debaters' statements of which arguments are better.

See also: PARADIGM, TABULA RASA

gap inherency

Definition: An approach to inherency that shows the present system has not taken any action on a problem.

Example: Local governments have not done anything to deal with the synthetic drug problem, mostly because the problem is just now being discovered.

See also: EXISTENTIAL INHERENCY, INHERENCY

generalization

Definition: To argue that specific incidents make a general rule.

Example: Because sex education has worked in St. Paul, Minnesota, and Pomona, California, sex education will work throughout the country.

See also: EXTRAPOLATION, INDUCTION, REASONING

generic argument

Definition: A general argument that applies to many arguments, plans, or value examples.

Example: A *generic argument* against a value that supports arms sales to Canada would be "Military sales are generally bad."

Usage: That's a generic argument. *(That argument is general; it does not show that it applies to specific cases.)* Get the generics. *(Get the generic arguments, the arguments that apply to many cases.)*

See also: CLASSIFICATION, GENERIC DISADVANTAGE, GENERIC VALUE OBJECTION

generic disadvantage

Definition: A general argument that shows many plans would cause harm.

Example: A *generic disadvantage* might show that any tax increase is bad. For example:

I. A tax increase will cause economic hardship.
   A. Tax increases hurt the economy.
   B. Hurting the economy will cause hardship.

This disadvantage could be used against any plan that calls for any kind of taxes.

See also: CLASSIFICATION, GENERIC ARGUMENT, GENERIC VALUE OBJECTION

generic value objection

Definition: A general argument that shows many value examples would reject the resolution.

Example: A *generic value objection* on the resolution "RESOLVED: That a tax increase would damage the economy" would be "Any tax increase will cause economic hardship."

See also: CLASSIFICATION, GENERIC ARGUMENT, GENERIC DISADVANTAGE

generics

See: GENERIC ARGUMENT

gestures

Definition: A speaker's physical movements during a speech that convey a meaning.

Example: Holding up two fingers to indicate two of something. Pounding on the table to emphasize a point.
See also: DELIVERY, SPEAKER

go down
Definition: To lose.
Usage: Who went down? *(Which teams lost their debates?)* Did you go down? *(Did you lose that debate?)*
See also: LOSE, WIN

go down to
Definition: A statement that indicates the speaker will now address a point that was made later in a previous speech and is therefore written lower down on a flowsheet.
Usage: Go down to the B-2 point. *(Please direct your attention to the arguments lower on your flowsheet that relate to the argument organized as the B-2 point.)*
See also: FLOW (1), FLOW (2), FLOWSHEET, GOING OFFCASE, GOING TO CASESIDE, GOING TO PLANSIDE, ON

goal
Definition: A desired objective.
Example: A *goal* of President Reagan's foreign policy was to stop communism. A *goal* in an affirmative case might be to achieve full employment.
Synonym: OBJECTIVE
See also: CRITERIA, GOALS-CRITERIA CASE, VALUE

goals-criteria case
Definition: A type of affirmative case that states a desired objective and shows how the present system does not meet the goal and how the affirmative plan would better meet the objective.
Example: A very basic outline of a *goals-criteria case.*
 I. The goal should be to reduce poverty as much as possible.
 II. The present system will not reduce poverty significantly. (The affirmative then presents their plan to guarantee a minimum income to everyone.)
 III. Guaranteed minimum income will significantly reduce poverty.
See also: AFFIRMATIVE CASE, CASE STRUCTURES, CRITERIA, CRITERIA CASE, GOAL

God terms

Definition: Words or phrases with positive connotations.

Example: Democracy, freedom, growth, liberty.

Antonym: DEVIL TERMS

going offcase

Definition: A statement that indicates the speaker will now begin making arguments that deal directly with the negative offcase. Offcase arguments are arguments that do not directly apply to the affirmative case. Offcase arguments are the negative case. For example, value objections are offcase arguments.

Usage: I'm going offcase. *(I will now discuss the offcase arguments, so you should begin looking at your notes of the offcase arguments—the offcase flow.)*

See also: FLOW (1), FLOW (2), FLOWSHEET, GO DOWN TO, GOING TO CASESIDE, GOING TO PLANSIDE, OFFCASE, PLANSIDE

going to caseside

Definition: A statement that indicates the speaker will now begin arguments that directly deal with the affirmative case. Caseside is the arguments which directly apply to the affirmative case, like significance in policy debate or criteria in value debate.

Usage: I'm going to caseside. *(I will now discuss the caseside arguments, so you should begin looking at your notes of the caseside arguments—the caseside flow.)*

See also: FLOW (1), FLOW (2), FLOWSHEET, GO DOWN TO, GOING OFFCASE, GOING TO PLANSIDE, ON

going to planside

Definition: A statement that indicates the speaker will now begin arguments that deal with the affirmative plan. Planside is the arguments, like disadvantages, that apply to the plan.

Usage: I'm going to planside. *(I will now discuss the planside arguments, so you should begin looking at your notes on the planside arguments—the planside flow.)*

See also: FLOW (1), FLOW (2), FLOWSHEET, GO DOWN TO, GOING OFFCASE, GOING TO CASESIDE, ON

government documents

Definition: Transcripts of government studies and hearings distributed by the government.

Example: *Hearings of the Foreign Relations Committee: El Salvador and Human Rights.*

See also: GOVERNMENT PUBLICATIONS

government publications

Definition: The written materials distributed by the government.

Example: In the United States, *government publications* include, for example, the *Congressional Record,* which has transcripts of congressional speeches, and government documents that include transcripts of government studies and hearings.

See also: GOVERNMENT DOCUMENTS, CONGRESSIONAL DIGEST, CONGRESSIONAL RECORD

gross

Definition: The amount gained without considering losses; the amount lost without considering gains.

Antonym: NET

See also: COMPARISON, WEIGH

gross generalization

Definition: A statement that does not account for exceptions.

Example: The statement "All of the presidents have been good" is probably a *gross generalization* since some presidents have not been good.

See also: GENERALIZATION, GROSS, HASTY GENERALIZATION

ground (1)

Definition: The position or positions that a team may argue for or against. The affirmative ground is usually the positions supporting the topic, while the negative ground is usually everything else.

Example: On a topic "RESOLVED: That U.S. policy in Africa should change," the affirmative *ground* would be any position supporting change in U.S. policy in Africa; the negative *ground* would be any position that did not support change in U.S. policy in Africa.

Usage:	They are giving us no ground. *(They are making arguments or taking positions that do not allow for us to respond because any response would support their position, their ground.)*
See also:	DEBATABILITY

ground (2)

Definition:	The position(s) or side given presumption.
See:	PRESUMPTION

grouping

Definition:	To respond to several arguments at the same time.
Example:	A team makes three arguments: First, sports cars are dangerous because they go too fast; second, sports cars can kill because they are easily smashed in accidents; and third, sports cars have been shown to have higher death rates. A speaker may choose to *group* these arguments and respond: "Please *group* their arguments that show sports cars are dangerous. I will have two responses. . . ."
Synonym:	LUMP
See also:	REFUTATION

H

handbook
Definition: A book filled with evidence. Some handbooks include analysis on the resolution or tips on how to debate.
See also: EVIDENCE, RESEARCH

harms
Definition: An undesirable result of a problem, policy, or value.
Example: Unemployment risks the *harms* of increased suicides, increased crime, and loss of a sense of worth. Jailing criminals leads to overcrowded prisons and risks the *harms* of riots and security guard killings. The value of stopping communism may risk the *harm* of war.
See also: SIGNIFICANCE

hasty generalization
Definition: To show that a speaker's arguments or examples do not prove a general rule; to argue a plan or value example is not topical because it is not representative of the resolution.
Example: A speaker that argues a program that worked in a small town will work throughout the country may be making a *hasty generalization*. A case that discusses the harms of one small weapon on a resolution "RESOLVED: That most weapons are on balance dangerous" would probably be a

hasty generalization because one small weapon is too insignificant to be considered "most weapons."

See also: FALLACY, GENERALIZATION, INDUCTION, ISOLATED EXAMPLE, REPRESENTATIVE, TYPICALITY

hearsay
Definition: Evidence based on secondhand information.
Example: According to a source close to the President, Medicare benefits will be cut.
See also: PRIMARY RESEARCH

heckling
Definition: Occurs when an audience member shouts or argues during a speaker's speech.
Example: During Hubert Humphrey's 1968 campaign for the presidency, Vietnam War protestors often *heckled* his speeches by yelling out anti-Vietnam War statements. During an academic debate, an audience member might *heckle* by speaking out against a debater.
Usage: Stop heckling her. *(Stop snickering, whispering, or making rude faces at the speaker.)*
See also: ETHICS, HECKLING FORMAT DEBATE

heckling format debate
Definition: A debate in which speakers are questioned and challenged by the audience and their opponents during their speeches.
See also: DEBATE FORMATS

high-high
Definition: Matching the debate teams with the best win-loss record and best speaker points against each other.
See also: HIGH-LOW, MATCHING

high-low
Definition: Matching of debate teams, placing the team with highest speaker points and best win-loss record against a team with the least speaker points but the same win-loss record.
Example: After four rounds at a tournament, teams have the following win-loss records and speaker points:

A: 2–0 108	E: 1–1 101	I: 1–1 88	M: 0–2 102
B: 2–0 102	F: 1–1 98	J: 1–1 86	N: 0–2 91
C: 2–0 99	G: 1–1 90	K: 1–1 78	O: 0–2 80
D: 2–0 90	H: 1–1 89	L: 1–1 66	P: 0–2 59

With high-high matching, A would debate B, C would debate D, E would debate F, and so on. With high-low matching, A would debate D, B would debate C, E would debate L, F would debate K, and so on.

See also: HIGH-HIGH, MATCHING

high school debate
Definition: Academic debate among high school students.
See also: ACADEMIC DEBATE, COLLEGE DEBATE, DEBATE, HIGH SCHOOL POLICY DEBATE, LINCOLN-DOUGLAS DEBATE

high school policy debate
Definition: Academic debate among high school students using a policy topic.
Example: Two high school teams that debate the topic "RESOLVED: That the United States should change its policy in Africa," are engaged in *high school policy debate.*
See also: LINCOLN-DOUGLAS DEBATE, NDT DEBATE, POLICY DEBATE, RESOLUTION OF POLICY

humor
Definition: Using jokes or one's demeanor to cause an audience to smile or laugh.
Usage: You have a good sense of humor. *(You have a good ability to laugh off difficult situations; or You have a good ability to make people laugh.)*
See also: DELIVERY, STYLE

hypothesis testing
Definition: A view that debates require the affirmative to prove the hypothesis—the resolution. A hypothesis-testing judge, generally, gives presumption to the negative because the affirmative must prove the resolution. However, any negative positions or arguments also must be proven since they are

hypotheses needing proof. Conditional arguments are acceptable. Counterwarrants may be more likely to be accepted because the affirmative may need to prove the whole resolution and not just examples of it. The negative may advance any issue they feel will disprove the resolution. The affirmative needs to defeat any issue advanced by the negative.

See also: PARADIGM, SYSTEMS ANALYSIS

hypothetical

Definition: To take or suggest a position that one does not necessarily support.

Usage: Hypothetically, one could just implement the affirmative's nationwide plan in the one state where there is a bee problem and that would solve this whole problem. *(We the negative, without committing to it, argue that a one-state plan would be better than a nationwide plan to deal with this bee problem. We do this to show that the affirmative plan is unnecessary because the problem is in only one state.)*

See also: CONDITIONALITY, GAMESPLAYER, HYPOTHESIS TESTING

hypothetical counterplan

Definition: A counterplan that is hypothetically advocated.

See: HYPOTHETICAL

I

if-then argument

Definition: An argument that reads, "If one argument is true, then another is true."

Example: *"If* there is a large number of people who do not receive medical care now because of cost, *then* giving free medical care will greatly increase the number of patients at hospitals."

See also: CONDITIONALITY, EITHER-OR ARGUMENT

ignore (an issue or argument)

Definition: To not respond to or not consider an issue or argument.

Example: In a debate, a negative team might argue that the affirmative plan would cause a war. The affirmative team would ignore the war argument if they did not respond to it. The judge would *ignore* the argument if he or she did not consider it in his or her decision.

See also: CLASH, DISCO, DROP, REFUTATION

impact (1)

Definition: An explanation of how a piece of evidence proves an argument; an explanation of how an argument proves or disproves a stand on an issue or the resolution; a warrant.

Example: *Claim:* Companies won't use performance supervision.

Evidence:

> Jan Muczyk and Brian Heshizer, Professors of Management, Cleveland State University, August 1986, p. 103.
> "Designing, implementing and maintaining sound performance evaluations systems requires time, continuous effort and money—a price that many organizations are unwilling to pay."

Impact: So, because of the cost and implementation time, companies won't use performance supervision; or So, because companies won't use performance supervision, we need drug testing; or So, because companies won't use performance supervision, all of the negative arguments showing it works are irrelevant.

Synonym: WARRANT

See also: ARGUMENT, BACKING, IMPACT (2), WARRANT

impact (2)

Definition: A type of argument that explicitly shows the importance of a main argument or an issue; an argument that shows why an issue or argument is a voting issue. Impacts are frequently used in topicality, value objection, and disadvantage arguments. Impacts are usually included in the last part of an argument.

Example: An outline of the *impact* of a topicality argument might look like this:

C. Topicality is a voting issue.
    1. The affirmative must affirm the topic.
    2. It would be unfair to the negative.

On a disadvantage or value objection, the *impacts* are like harms and are designed to outweigh an affirmative advantage or support and might look like this:

C. Increasing tensions would be disastrous.
    1. It would risk war.
    2. Millions could be killed.
    3. Risking war is the worst possible situation.

See also: DISADVANTAGE, IMPACT (1), TOPICALITY, VALUE OBJEC-
TION

implement
Definition: To put into action; to pass into law. An affirmative in a pol-
icy debate urges implementation of its plan.
See also: FIAT, SHOULD-WOULD FALLACY

impromptu (1)
Definition: To deliver a speech with virtually no preparation.
Example: A debater might make up responses against an opponent's
arguments right off the top of his head. This would be an
impromptu response because the debater made the response
without research or preparation.
See also: DELIVERY, EXTEMPORANEOUS (1)

impromptu (2)
Definition: A speech event in which a speaker speaks on one of three
topics after preparing, usually for two minutes at most.
See also: EXTEMPORANEOUS (2)

in
Definition: To compete in elimination rounds.
Usage: Are you in? *(Will you compete in the final rounds?* or *Did you
have a good enough win-loss record to compete in the elimination
rounds?)*
Synonym: OUT (1)
See also: ELIMINATION ROUNDS, OUT (2)

inconsistency
Definition: The degree to which positions are incompatible; the inabil-
ity of arguments to work together; arguments that do not
contradict but appear to support differing positions.
Example: To argue that cigarettes cause few cancers is *inconsistent* with
the argument that cigarettes should be banned because,
while the arguments do not contradict, one appears to support cigarettes, the other does not.
See also: CONDITIONALITY, CONSISTENCY, CONTRADICTION, DI-
LEMMA, HYPOTHESIS TESTING

increment
Definition: A small amount; an increase.
Usage: I give the affirmative an increment of their advantage. *(I feel the affirmative will gain a small amount of their advantage.)*
See also: PROBABILITY, RISK, SIGNIFICANCE

incrementalism
Definition: A position that shows that the present system is slowly changing.
Example: Instead of an immediate national toxic waste cleanup, a negative could argue that an *incremental* approach, relying on slower and more flexible cleanup changes, would be superior.
See also: INHERENCY, PERMANENCE

independent
Definition: Distinct from; an argument stating that if Argument X is won, Argument X alone will win the round.
Example: A solar power plan might gain two *independent*—two distinct—advantages of decreasing the threat of oil shortages and of decreasing nuclear power dangers.
Usage: This value objection is an independent voting issue. *(This argument that shows that the affirmative value does not support the resolution is so important that the negative should win the debate even if the affirmative wins all the other issues.)*
See also: DISCO, SEVER, VOTING ISSUE

index
Definition: An organized listing of the contents of a book, file, or library materials.
Example: Files of evidence have *indexes* telling debaters where to find what evidence. A book has an *index* telling where to find a particular issue in the book.
See also: CARD CATALOG, FILE

index cards
Definition: A 3″ × 5″ or 4″ × 6″ blank piece of paper upon which evidence is placed.
See also: CARD, EVIDENCE

indict

Definition: To cite fault with; to show to be bad.

Example: A team might *indict* Elliot Abrams because he lied to Congress several times about aid to Iran and the Nicaraguan Contras.

Usage: We indicted their evidence. *(We showed their evidence was biased or was based on inaccurate information.)* Where are our indict briefs? *(Where is our evidence on sheets of paper that shows a source is bad?)*

See also: BIAS

induction

Definition: To reason that an example proves a general rule.

Example: Because this Toyota does not work, most Toyotas do not work. Because drug education failed at two midwestern schools, it would probably not work throughout the nation.

Antonym: DEDUCTION

See also: EXTRAPOLATION, GENERALIZATION, INFERENCE, REASONING, SPECIALIZATION

inexperienced division

Definition: A group of debate teams which have not debated many times who compete against each other at a debate tournament.

See also: DIVISION, TOURNAMENT

inference

Definition: To make a conclusion based on an argument or evidence.

Example: A person who notices bugs are dying in a hot light fixture might *infer* that the heat of the fixture causes the bugs to die. A debater might *infer* that because a plan will increase economic development it will also increase pollution.

See also: BACKING, EXTRAPOLATION, REASONING, WARRANT

information

Definition: Knowledge about something; evidence.

Usage: Where did you get that information? *(What book, article, or person provided you with that knowledge?)* Do you have any information to support that point? *(Do you have any evidence to support that point?)*

See also: EVIDENCE, RESEARCH

Infotrack

Definition: A computerized listing of a library's books, documents, journals, magazines, and other materials.

See also: CARD CATALOG

inherency

Definition: The issue of whether the present system will solve the problem or achieve the advantage.

Example: Here is a mini-debate on the issue of *inherency.*

> *Affirmative:* The present system's use of private insurance and low cost medical care clinics is not able to provide enough care to the poor, so we need to offer free care to all.

> *Negative:* The present system is able to give the poor enough care through private insurance and low cost medical care clinics, so we don't need free care for everybody.

Usage: They didn't have any inherency. *(The affirmative did not show that the present system was unable to solve the problem.)* We ran inherency against them. *(The negative argued that changing the system was not needed because the present system would solve the problem.)*

Note: Inherency is not whether the affirmative plan can or will be passed (see SHOULD-COULD FALLACY).

See also: BARRIER, EXISTENTIAL INHERENCY, INHERENT, INHERENT BARRIER, PLANSIDE BARRIER, STATUS QUO, STOCK ISSUES

inherency-solvency or inherency-disadvantage dilemma

Definition: Occurs when a team's inherency arguments contradict their disadvantage or solvency arguments.

Example: The negative team argues, against a plan for sex education, that many states have effective sex education programs and then argues that sex education programs are bad.

See also: DILEMMA, INHERENCY

inherent barrier

Definition: An attitude, law, program, or policy that prevents the present system from solving the problem or achieving the advantage.

Example: The *inherent barrier* that prevents the end of pesticide-caused environmental damage may be the attitude of the present system, which promotes chemical pesticides. The *inherent barrier* to solving the small farm bankruptcy problem may be the laws and programs that overemphasize large farms.

See also: BARRIER, CASESIDE BARRIER, INHERENCY, INHERENT BARRIER, PLANSIDE BARRIER

inherent change

Definition: A change in law, program, or policy; an affirmative plan.

Example: A plan that would end prison sentences is an *inherent change* in the law.

See also: INHERENCY, MINOR REPAIR, PLAN

inside-outside

Definition: Occurs when the first affirmative speaker does the first affirmative constructive and the second affirmative rebuttal (outsides), and the second affirmative speaker does the second affirmative constructive and the first affirmative rebuttal (insides).

Synonym: FLIP-FLOP

See also: EMORY SWITCH, INSIDES

insides

Definition: The second affirmative speaker, who does the second affirmative constructive and the first affirmative rebuttal.

See also: EMORY SWITCH, INSIDE-OUTSIDE

institute (1)

See: CAMP

institute (2)

See: IMPLEMENT

instrumental value

Definition: A type of value that is a means.

Example: The *instrumental value* of democracy might lead to a terminal value of decreasing revolutions and wars.

See also: TERMINAL VALUE, VALUE

intent

Definition: The unstated goal or objective of a plan or statement.

Usage: Legislative intent—all planks will be interpreted by the affirmative. *(The affirmative will explain any confusing portions of the plan and any unstated goals or objectives of the plan.)*

See also: PLAN, PLANK

intermediate division

Definition: A group of debate teams with some experience and some success who compete against one another in a tournament.

See also: DIVISION, TOURNAMENT

interscholastic

Definition: Between different schools.

Example: When Ardmore High School debates Lakeway High School, the debate is an *interscholastic debate.*

See also: ACADEMIC DEBATE, INTRASCHOLASTIC

intervention

Definition: Occurs when a judge uses an argument not made in the debate or ignores an important argument in his or her decision.

Example: A judge would *intervene* against a plan to legalize marijuana if she voted against the plan because she was against legalizing marijuana, even though the affirmative had shown that this plan would reduce drug use and decrease corruption and the negative made no arguments against the plan.

Usage: That judge is an interventionist. *(That judge will make decisions based on his own arguments, not the debaters'.)*

See also: CRITIC OF ARGUMENT, PRESUMPTION, TABULA RASA

intrascholastic

Definition: Within a school. Intrascholastic debate occurs between teams from the same school competing against each other; for example, in a class.

See also: ACADEMIC DEBATE, INTERSCHOLASTIC

intrinsic
Definition: A primary result of a policy or value; a result that would occur even if alternative action occurred.
Example: An *intrinsic* argument is "The plan to ban tobacco production will economically dislocate tobacco growers" because there is essentially nothing that a plan could do to prevent the economic dislocation. A *non-intrinsic* argument is "Banning tobacco production will increase unemployment among tobacco growers." A plan could offer the growers other jobs or give them an opportunity to grow other products.
See also: COMPETITIVENESS, DISADVANTAGE, INHERENCY

introduction
Definition: The beginning of a speech. Introductions to speeches in debate usually include the team's position and main reason the team deserves to win.
See also: CASE, CONCLUSION

invention
Definition: The creation of a speech or case. Debaters engage in the process of invention when they get an idea for, research, organize, and write a case.
See also: RESEARCH

irrelevant
Definition: Not applicable to an issue, argument, plan, or value.
Example: An *irrelevant* response to the argument "War propaganda increases the chance of war" would be "People do make peaceful messages."
Usage: That argument is irrelevant. *(That argument does not apply to the issue and therefore should be ignored.)*
See also: RED HERRING

is-ought fallacy
Definition: To falsely assume that "is" means "ought."
Example: An *is-ought fallacy* on the resolution "RESOLVED: That U.S. foreign policy is supporting human rights" would be the argument "U.S. foreign policy ought to support human

rights." The argument should instead argue U.S. foreign policy is supporting human rights.

See also: FALLACY, SHOULD-COULD FALLACY, SHOULD-WOULD FALLACY

isolated example

Definition: An event or item that does not prove the general rule.

Example: To prove that drinking water is unsafe throughout the country, the debaters used an *isolated example:* they argued that one town has unsafe drinking water.

See also: EXTRAPOLATION, HASTY GENERALIZATION, INDUCTION

issue

Definition: An area of argument that needs to be addressed in order to prove or disprove a resolution.

Example: The stock *issues* in a policy debate are topicality, significance, inherency, solvency, and disadvantages. The *issues* in a debate about a mandatory pledge of allegiance might be freedom of choice, patriotism, and the constitutionality of a mandatory pledge.

Usage: This is an important issue. *(This general argument is crucial to winning or losing the debate.)*

See also: ARGUMENT (2), STOCK ISSUES, SYSTEMS ANALYSIS

J

"J"

See: JUSTIFICATION

jargon

Definition: Words and phrases that are understood only to experts in the field that uses those words and phrases.

Example: "This takeout beats the counterplan cold." This is *jargon* because only those who are experienced in debate will know what "takeout," "beats," and "counterplan" mean.

See also: COMMUNICATION, STYLE

jettison

See: SEVER

judge

Definition: The person who decides which debate team won the debate. There is usually one judge who decides who wins a preliminary debate, and three judges who decide who wins elimination rounds of debate. The judge listens to a debate, takes notes and writes down comments for improvement, and then writes down who won and why.

Synonym: CRITIC

See also: AUDIENCE, CONSTRUCTIVE CRITICISM, PARADIGM

judicial notice

Definition: An argument that does not require evidence since the judge knows the argument to be valid; common sense.

Example: Ronald Reagan was president in 1987. The United States has fifty states.

See also: EVIDENCE, SUPPORT

judicial paradigm

Definition: A view that debates are like trials. The defendant (usually the negative) is the present system or present beliefs. The prosecutor (usually the affirmative) is for changing the present system or present beliefs. The defendant is given a strong presumption, just like a defendant in a court trial is considered innocent until proven guilty. The affirmative wins if they can demonstrate that there is a serious and inherent problem with the present system or present beliefs and if they can show that their plan or value alternative is superior and appropriate to deal with the problem.

See also: PARADIGM, PRESUMPTION

junior division

Definition: A group of debate teams composed of freshmen or sophomores, or of juniors and seniors with less than one year of experience, who compete against each other at debate tournaments.

See also: DIVISION, TOURNAMENT

jurisdiction

Definition: The topical cases or plans upon which a judge may make a decision.

Example: A plan for legalization of cocaine on a resolution "RESOLVED: That the United States should legalize marijuana" would probably not be in a judge's *jurisdiction* because cocaine is not marijuana and is therefore not topical.

Usage: Topicality is a jurisdictional issue. *(Topicality is an issue of what the judge can and cannot rule upon. If the affirmative is not topical, then the affirmative loses because the case is not within the judge's jurisdiction and should be handled by someone else.)*

See also: IMPACT (2), TOPICALITY, VOTING ISSUE

jurisprudential model of argument
See: TOULMIN MODEL OF ARGUMENT

justification (1)
Definition: A topicality argument that argues the affirmative has not given reason to support the resolution.
Example: If the resolution was "RESOLVED: That the United States should increase aid to foreign countries," and the affirmative plan increased aid to foreign countries and was financed by taxing chemical companies, the negative could make a *justification* argument if the affirmative cited advantages only to taxing chemical companies. The negative could argue that the affirmative had not justified increasing aid to foreign countries since this tax is not topical.
See also: EXTRA-TOPICALITY, INTRINSIC, JUSTIFICATION (2), JUSTIFICATION (3), TOPICALITY

justification (2)
Definition: A topicality argument that argues there is a superior alternative to the affirmative plan.
Example: The negative could make a *justification* argument against an affirmative that supports a plan to have the United States take an action in Central America. The negative could argue that a better way to do this would be to have the United States act cooperatively with the Organization of American States.
Note: Essentially, justification (2) is a counterplan that is not necessarily competitive and for that reason is considered illegitimate by some.
See also: COUNTERPLAN, JUSTIFICATION (1), JUSTIFICATION (3), TOPICALITY

justification (3)
Definition: A topicality argument that shows the affirmative plan (policy debate) or value example (value debate) is not a representative example of the resolution.
Example: The negative could make a *justification* argument against a plan that mandated sex education in elementary and high schools under the topic "RESOLVED: That the nation's elementary and high schools should have sex education" if

the affirmative could not show that sex education in elementary schools was good. The negative could argue that, even though the affirmative showed sex education was good in high schools, the affirmative had not justified having sex education in elementary schools, and therefore had not justified the resolution which supported both elementary and high school sex education.

Note: Since the affirmative, at a minimum, still supports the topic, some judges do not consider this a voting issue.

Synonym: SUB-TOPICALITY

See also: JUSTIFICATION (1), JUSTIFICATION (2), TOPICALITY

K

key

Definition: Important.

Usage: This is key. *(This argument is very important for making a decision in the debate.)*

See also: VOTING ISSUE

key terms

Definition: Important words or phrases in the resolution or in a case.

Example: In the resolution "RESOLVED: That the federal government should ban cigarettes," the *key terms* would be "federal government," "ban," and "cigarettes." "That," "the," and "should" are unlikely to be as important in determining what is a topical or non-topical plan to support.

See also: RESOLUTION, TOPICALITY

kicked out

Definition: To have argued.

Usage: I kicked out six disads against that draft resister case. *(I argued that a draft resister plan would cause six disadvantages.)*

See also: KICKS IN, TAKE OUT

kicks in

Definition: As a result of this argument, another argument or issue applies.

Usage: Because we show that insulating homes will lead to increased levels of home radon gas, the radon gas harms kick in. *(Because we have shown that insulating homes leads to increased home radon gas, our previous argument that showed radon gas is harmful now applies.)*

See also: TAKE OUT

kicks out

See: TAKE OUT

L

label
See: CLAIM

lay judge
Definition: A person without much debate experience who decides who won a debate. Debaters should emphasize more persuasive, slower communication and develop clear arguments to convince a lay judge.
See also: COMMUNICATION, DELIVERY, JUDGE, PARADIGM, SKILLS JUDGE

leading question
Definition: A question that leads a respondent to make a damaging answer.
Example: A questioner wants to argue that increased trade would be bad, so she asks the *leading question*, "So, you say your plan will lead to increased trade, right?"
See also: ANSWER, CROSS-EXAMINATION, QUESTION, QUESTIONER, RESPONDENT, RESPONSE

legal advocacy
Definition: A speech that requires speakers to make an argument supporting the defense or prosecution in a legal case.

Example: The speaker might be asked to argue for or against banning textbooks that contain information considered antireligious by some groups.

legislative debate

Definition: Debate that occurs in the legislature. The debates are usually a series of speeches that support or reject a bill in Congress. The speakers usually respond to general arguments made against their position, and rarely make direct responses to other speakers' arguments.

See also: ARGUMENT (2), AUDIENCE DEBATE, DEBATE, DISPUTE

Library of Congress

Definition: The government office that stores and organizes all copyrighted written material, like books and magazines. Books in a library are often organized into the Library of Congress (LOC) system. The books are ordered numerically and alphabetically with call numbers like "BF 721 I473."

See also: DEWEY DECIMAL SYSTEM

likelihood

Definition: The probability, chances, that an event will occur.

Example: There is a 14 percent *likelihood* that the United Nations will collapse, if there is a 14 percent chance that the United Nations will collapse because of infighting.

Usage: The likelihood that selling tractors to farmers in the Midwest will cause nuclear war is very low. *(The chance that selling tractors to midwestern farmers will cause nuclear war is very low.)*

Synonyms: PLAUSIBILITY, PROBABILITY

Lincoln-Douglas debate

Definition: A type of debate in which one debater argues against another. A Lincoln-Douglas debate usually has the following speeches: Affirmative constructive (six or seven minutes), negative constructive (seven or eight minutes), first affirmative rebuttal (four minutes), negative rebuttal (six minutes), and second affirmative rebutal (three minutes). The debates are usually communication-oriented and address a value proposition.

See also: CEDA DEBATE, HIGH SCHOOL POLICY DEBATE, OFF-TOPIC DEBATE, POLICY DEBATE

linear
Definition: To increase or decrease proportionately
Example: A *linear* argument might be "For each percentage increase in taxes, the economic damage will increase." A *non-linear* argument might be "The economy will be damaged only if the percentage of taxes hits a certain level."
See also: ASSOCIATION, BRINK, CAUSAL RELATIONSHIP, RELATIONSHIP

link
Definition: One event causes another.
See: CAUSAL LINK

links
Definition: The arguments in a disadvantage that show the plan will cause or increase a problem; the arguments in a value objection that show that the value object or value example will cause or increase a problem.
Example: The *links* of an "increased risk of war" disadvantage against a plan that increases defense spending might be:
B. Links: Increased defense spending increases the risk of war.
   1. Increased defense spending creates a dangerous U.S.-Soviet arms race.
   2. Increased defense spending creates a military mindset in the United States.
   3. Increased defense spending creates dangerous new weapons.
See also: CAUSAL LINK, DISADVANTAGE, VALUE OBJECTION

literal analogy
Definition: A real comparison between two alike items or events.
Example: "U.S. military involvement in Central America is just like U.S. military involvement in Vietnam."
See also: FIGURATIVE ANALOGY

loaded argument

Definition: An argument that is phrased to make opposition to the argument sound bad.

Example: "This missile is a peacekeeper, and anyone who doesn't support this missile is against peace and against America."

See also: AD HOMINEM ATTACK, FALLACY, LOGIC, REASONING

logic

Definition: The use of reason to make arguments about facts, values, and policies.

See also: REASONING

logical reasoning

See: REASONING

logos

Definition: The use of logic in a speech.

See: LOGIC

lose

Definition: To not win; to be the team that the judge does not vote for in a debate.

See also: WIN

lump

See: GROUP

M

macro

Definition: Viewed from a large or holistic level.

Example: Instead of looking at a pesticide problem in one incident in a farming community, the *macro* approach would examine a pesticide problem all over the country. A plan with a *macro* approach to pesticide problems would not suggest a detailed program for each place that uses pesticides, but rather would suggest an overall approach; for example, using biological pesticides instead of chemical pesticides.

Antonym: MICRO

major premise

Definition: The main assumption of a syllogism.

Example: *Major Premise:* If a proposed building is over four stories high, then it shall not be built.

Minor Premise: The proposed Z building is five stories high.

Conclusion: The Z building shall not be built.

See also: ENTHYMEME, IF-THEN ARGUMENT, SYLLOGISM

mandates

Definition: The section or plank of an affirmative plan that states what the affirmative wants to see put into action.

Example: Plank Two: *Mandates.* The affirmative plan will enact the following:
A. A ban on lead in any new plumbing.
B. Removal of all lead piping within ten years.
C. Make health care and education available to all in areas with piping containing high amounts of lead.

See also: PLAN, PLANK, SPIKE

manuscript
Definition: A fully written-out speech. The first affirmative constructive is often a neatly typed-out *manuscript.*

See also: CASE, ORATORY

matching
Definition: The process of assigning who debates whom. At many tournaments, during the first two or three debate rounds, teams from different regions are matched against each other. During later rounds, teams with similar records are usually matched against each other (for example, a team with a 3-0 record would debate another team with a 3-0 record and a 2-1 team would debate another team with a 2-1 record).

Synonym: PAIRING
See also: HIGH-HIGH, HIGH-LOW, MISMATCHING

maverick judge
Definition: A judge who makes unpredictable decisions.
Example: The *maverick* judge was the only one in the entire room, including both teams, the audience, and the other two judges, who felt the affirmative won.
Usage: You can never tell which way that maverick will vote. (*You can never tell what decision that judge who often votes differently will make.*)
See also: AUDIENCE ANALYSIS, JUDGE, PARADIGM, TURKEY

meatball
See: GENERIC DISADVANTAGE

mechanism

Definition: A loophole in a law, program, or policy that makes a circumvention argument possible; what someone would use to put a policy into action.

Example: A *mechanism,* a loophole, to get around a plan that bans government arms sales to the Contras in Nicaragua would be to sell arms privately to the Contras. *Mechanisms* to solve the illiteracy problem would be, for example, remedial reading programs, school assistance programs, and English as a Second Language programs.

See also: CIRCUMVENTION, INHERENCY, MINOR REPAIR, MOTIVE, PLAN

mega-impact argument

Definition: An argument with extremely large impact; an argument that addresses an extremely important issue.

Example: A disadvantage that argues a plan will cause nuclear war, an advantage that saves the world from environmental destruction, and a value objection that shows a total loss of democracy are all *mega-impact arguments.*

Synonym: BIG IMPACT

See also: GENERIC DISADVANTAGE, GENERIC VALUE OBJECTION

memorize

Definition: To remember, word for word, a speech.

Usage: Memorize the case. *(Practice the case until you can recite it without looking at the case.)*

See also: FIRST AFFIRMATIVE CONSTRUCTIVE, MANUSCRIPT

methodology

Definition: The statement of how a study was conducted.

Example: The study included 1,000 children and over 300 elementary schools. The children and schools were representative of children and schools throughout the country. Students were given psychological interviews; teachers were asked to fill out surveys.

Usage: What was the methodology of your study? *(How was the study that you cited conducted? Describe how it was done.)*

See also: EMPIRICAL

Michigan style debate

Definition: Debate format that includes questioning by the debaters and the audience.

See also: DEBATE FORMATS

micro

Definition: Viewed at a small, detailed level.

Example: A *micro* approach would be to examine, in detail, an area with an acid rain problem, instead of looking at acid rain throughout the world. A plan with a *micro* approach might ban a specific type of coal to prevent a specific type of acid rain.

Antonym: MACRO

minor premise

Definition: The argument in a syllogism that shows the condition of the major premise to be true.

Example: *Major Premise:* Books of over 10,000 words are good books.

Minor Premise: The book *Free to Choose* is 13,000 words long.

Conclusion: Free to Choose is a good book.

See also: CONCLUSION, ENTHYMEME, MAJOR PREMISE, SYLLO-GISM

minor repair

Definition: A minor modification in the present system to allow it to resolve a problem or help achieve an advantage; a small counterplan.

Example: If an affirmative completely overhauls the present education system, the negative could argue that only a *minor repair* to increase education funding is needed.

Usage: We can just minor repair that law by enforcing it. *(We can solve the problems associated with that law by enforcing it.)*

Note: With judges that consider a *minor repair* to be essentially a small counterplan, the negative needs to show that the *minor repair* is competitive and non-topical.

Synonym: ADJUSTMENT AND REPAIRS CASE

See also: COMPETITIVENESS, COUNTERPLAN, INHERENCY, MECHANISM, NON-TOPICAL

mismatching
Definition: To schedule teams with the best record against teams with the worst records.
Example: Matching a 5–0 team to hit a team with an 0–5 record would be *mismatching*.
Synonym: POWER PROTECT
See also: HIGH-HIGH, HIGH-LOW, MATCHING, POWER MATCHING

misrepresent
Definition: To present a piece of evidence or an argument inaccurately.
Example: Cutting out the word "no" from a piece of evidence would be a serious *misrepresentation* of evidence. To say that one's opponent supported communism because the opponent had argued that communism did not create as much harm as the affirmative had pointed out would be *misrepresenting* that opponent's position.
Synonym: DISTORT
See also: ETHICS, FABRICATION

missing an argument
Definition: To forget to respond to an argument.
Example: During a first affirmative rebuttal a speaker might *miss an argument* by not responding to a disadvantage argument.
Usage: You missed the topicality argument. *(You forgot to respond to the topicality argument.)*
See also: BURDEN OF REBUTTAL, BURDEN OF REJOINDER, CLASH, DROP, REFUTATION

mock trial
Definition: A pretend trial in which speakers act as lawyers would.
Example: A *mock trial* might concern a case about whether homosexual soldiers should be permitted in the army. One person would act as judge, others would act as jury members, others as stenographer and clerk, and others would act as lawyers. The lawyers would argue for and against the right of gay soldiers to be permitted in the army. After the *mock trial,* the judge or jury would make a decision on the case.
Synonym: MOOT COURT DEBATE
See also: JUDICIAL PARADIGM

modify

See: AMEND

modular case

Definition: A case with sections that can be changed, included, or excluded.

Example: A *modular* affirmative case might have six advantages. In different debates, the affirmative would use different advantages. In one debate, they might use just one advantage. In other debates, the affirmative might use two or three advantages and could use different advantages for each different debate.

See also: ALTERNATIVE JUSTIFICATION CASE, CASE STRUCTURES, INDEPENDENT

monotone

Definition: To speak without vocal variety.

Example: Some feel that Jimmy Carter's speaking is *monotone* because he drawls out his speeches without much variety and excitement.

See also: VOCAL INFLECTION, VOCAL TONE, VOCAL VARIETY

Montana style debate

Definition: A debate that pairs two-person teams. Each person gives a speech, questions and answers in cross-examination, and each team gives one rebuttal speech.

See also: DEBATE FORMATS

moot court debate

See: MOCK TRIAL

motion

Definition: A position put to vote in a student congress.

Example: A *motion* might call for a vote to support a resolution that calls for divestment in South Africa.

See also: STUDENT CONGRESS

motivational proofs

Definition: The use of appealing evidence to support an evaluative argument.

Example: American–Japanese trade is needed to help the world economy. Since helping the world economy is considered a good thing, America and Japan should continue their trade.

See also: TOULMIN MODEL OF ARGUMENT

motive

Definition: The desire to take action.

Example: The negative could argue there is a *motive* to circumvent a plan that banned arms transfers to the Contras because there are large numbers of people who are dedicated to the Contras. The negative could argue that many people in the education system are dedicated to ending illiteracy, and there is therefore a *motive* to solve the problem.

See also: CIRCUMVENTION, MECHANISM, MINOR REPAIR

multiple causality

Definition: Many causes.

Example: Acid rain may have *multiple causes*. For example, it may be caused by coal pollution, lack of lime in waters, natural pollution, sulfur emissions, and automobile emissions.

See also: ALTERNATE CAUSALITY, CAUSAL, MULTIPLE EFFECTS

multiple effects

Definition: Many results.

Example: A plan to use bilingual education has *multiple effects* because (an affirmative might argue) it might lead to greater literacy, better community relations, less stress for non-English speakers, and lower dropout rates.

See also: MULTIPLE CAUSALITY

multiple level arguments

Definition: At least two distinct arguments that account for opponent responses.

Example: "This plan will solve the poverty problem. If you simply look at our empirical studies, you know it will reduce poverty. If you assume that the poor will not take full advantage of the program, the plan will still reduce poverty to those who do take advantage, and we can try to educate the rest. Finally, even if you assume that the poor might not always like getting assistance, most want it and we at least give the poor a choice to get assistance."

See also: ANALYSIS, ARGUMENT (1), MULTIPLE RESPONSES, PRE-EMPTION

multiple responses

Definition: At least two distinct arguments that clash against an opposing argument.

Example: "There are six reasons why the plan would not help civil rights. First...."

See also: ANALYSIS, ARGUMENTS, MULTIPLE LEVEL ARGUMENTS

mutual exclusivity

Definition: The issue of whether it is impossible for a plan and a counterplan, or a value object and a value alternative, to exist at the same time.

Example: A *mutually exclusive* counterplan against a plan to give food aid might be one that banned giving food aid. A *mutually exclusive* value alternative against support for the United Nations would be to reject the United Nations.

See also: ALTERNATIVE, COUNTERPLAN, NET BENEFITS

N

NDT debate

Definition: College policy debate with four debaters. Constructive speeches are ten minutes; cross-examination is three minutes; rebuttals are five minutes. NDT stands for National Debate Tournament. NDT debate is usually quicker than other forms of debate and demands more research because of the large amounts of evidence required.

Usage: That was just like an NDT round. *(That debate was comparable in speed, analysis, type of arguments, or amount of evidence to an NDT debate.)*

See also: CEDA DEBATE, DEBATE FORMATS, HIGH SCHOOL POLICY DEBATE, LINCOLN-DOUGLAS DEBATE, NATIONAL DEBATE TOURNAMENT, POLICY DEBATE

NFL

See: NATIONAL FORENSIC LEAGUE

narrative paradigm

Definition: A view that debates are disputes where a judge chooses between two competing stories. A story is the position and supporting arguments presented by a team. A judge who uses the narrative paradigm examines the consistency of a team's argument story, and then determines which team's story is more persuasive based on the judge's own beliefs about the issue.

See also: CRITIC OF ARGUMENT, GAMESPLAYER, HYPOTHESIS TESTING, JUDICIAL PARADIGM, PARADIGM, SYSTEMS ANALYSIS, TABULA RASA

National Catholic High School League

Definition: A debate organization composed of Catholic high schools.
See also: NATIONAL FORENSIC LEAGUE

National Debate Tournament

Definition: The championship tournament for NDT debate; a tournament at which NDT debate is used. The National Debate Tournament was held at West Point until 1947. From then on, the tournament's location has varied each year. The tournament selects the best teams in the country to compete for the national championship. Many other tournaments are called National Debate Tournaments because they offer competition in the NDT form of debate, including, for example, the Northwestern, Emory, Heart of America, and University of Southern California tournaments.
See also: CEDA NATIONAL CHAMPIONSHIP, NDT DEBATE

National Developmental Conference of Forensics

Definition: An organization of high school and college speech and debate educators that establishes goals for the speech and debate community.
See also: CEDA, NATIONAL FORENSIC LEAGUE

National Forensic League

Definition: An organization of high school speech and debate teams throughout the United States.
See also: CEDA, NATIONAL DEVELOPMENTAL CONFERENCE OF FORENSICS

need

Definition: A significant problem that suggests a plan or advantage would be desirable. A *need* argument is usually presented by showing a significant problem.

Example: A serious pollution problem would be a *need* for a plan or advantage to reduce that serious pollution problem.

Synonym: SIGNIFICANCE

See also: ADVANTAGE, HARMS, PLAN

need-plan case

Definition: A case structure that shows there is a problem (a need), and a plan that can solve the problem.

Example: I. There is a serious need to deal with the farm belt problem.
    A. (Significance) Farms are going bankrupt.
    B. (Harms) Farmers are committing suicide and our economy is hurt.
    C. (Inherency) Current farm aid is inadequate.
Plan: Bail out all farmers with grants.

Solvency/Benefit: Grants will end the farm belt problem.

See also: CASE STRUCTURES

negative

Definition: The team that rejects the resolution and the affirmative case.

Example: On the resolution "RESOLVED: That the United States should not build the Strategic Defense Initiative ('Star Wars')," a *negative* would be for SDI and against any affirmative case that urges a ban on SDI.

Usage: We're on the negative next debate. *(We'll be arguing against the resolution next debate.)*

See also: AFFIRMATIVE, RESOLUTION

negative block

Definition: The second negative constructive and first negative rebuttal in team debates. During the negative block the negative team has twelve to fifteen minutes to build a strong attack against the affirmative. The first affirmative rebuttal then has only four to five minutes to respond to this negative block.

Synonym: BLOC

See also: DIVISION OF LABOR, FIRST NEGATIVE REBUTTAL, SECOND NEGATIVE CONSTRUCTIVE, SPEAKER DUTIES

net

Definition: On balance; after disadvantages are considered.

Example: The *net* advantage of a plan that saves 1,000 lives but also causes 233 deaths is 767 lives saved.

See also: GROSS

net benefits

Definition: The issue of whether it is desirable for a plan and a counterplan, or a value object and a value alternative, to exist at the same time. If it is desirable for the two to exist at the same time, the judge should ignore the counterplan or value alternative.

Example: A *net benefits* counterplan against a plan to increase bilingual education might use English as a Second Language (ESL) programs. The ESL counterplan would meet the *net benefits* standard if ESL and billingual programs together would increase the deficit too much, whereas ESL alone would not be that costly.

See also: COMPETITION, COUNTERPLAN, MUTUAL EXCLUSIVITY, PERMUTATION

net benefits case

Definition: An affirmative case structure that supports a plan because the net benefits of the affirmative plan outweigh the net benefits of the present system.

Example: I. The present use of plea bargaining is not beneficial.

    A. It increases injustice and releases dangerous criminals.

    B. It speeds the criminal justice system only a tiny bit.

Plan: Ban plea bargaining.

I. Banning plea bargaining would be beneficial.

    A. It would increase justice and prevent the release of dangerous criminals.

    B. It would not create more delays in the justice system.

See also: CASE STRUCTURES

nitpick

Definition: To make irritating, inconsequential responses to an argument.

Example: Here is a *nitpicky* response: "Our opponents argued that diamonds are expensive. Well, first, jewelry isn't. You can get cheap jewelry. Second, what's expensive? I mean, come on. Define it. Third, what is a diamond? They should define that, too. Fourth, I don't think they have proven their argument. I mean, all they show is that a diamond costs hundreds of dollars. So what?"

Usage: They're just nitpicking our arguments. *(They are making inconsequential responses to our arguments.)*

See also: CLASH, PRESS, REFUTATION

no show

Definition: Occurs when a debate team does not debate when scheduled to do so.

Example: Team X goes to their room to debate, and their opponents, team Y, never come to debate them.

Usage: Team 17S1 no showed! *(Team 17S1, which was supposed to debate, did not show up to debate.)*

See also: BYE, FORFEIT

no-needs case

Definition: A case structure that shows the present system gains no benefit and should therefore be changed.

Example: I. Current laws banning X cars in the area are no longer needed since X cars are no longer produced.

Plan: Get rid of the law banning X cars.

Synonym: UTILITY CASE

See also: CASE STRUCTURES

nonpolicy debate

Definition: Debates on resolutions of fact, value, and perhaps, quasi-policy. Debates on any topic without the words "should" or "ought to" are likely to be nonpolicy debates.

Example: Debate on resolutions like "RESOLVED: That human rights is an important foreign policy objective," "RESOLVED: That Ronald Reagan was a conservative president," and "RESOLVED: That drug testing is a good idea" would be *nonpolicy debates.*

See also: CEDA DEBATE, DEBATE, LINCOLN-DOUGLAS DEBATE, POLICY DEBATE, RESOLUTION OF FACT, RESOLUTION OF QUASI-POLICY, RESOLUTION OF VALUE

non sequitur
Definition: An argument with very weak or illogical support.
Example: Trains should be banned because trains go too fast and frequently get to their destination on time.
See also: FALLACY, LOGIC, REASONING

non-topical
Definition: To not be topical.
See: TOPICALITY

non-unique
Definition: Not unique.
See: UNIQUE

nonverbal communication
Definition: The messages a speaker conveys that are not the content of a speech. Nonverbal communication is conveyed by eye contact, gestures, vocal inflection and variety, and poise.
See also: COMMUNICATION, DELIVERY

notes
See: FLOW (1), FLOW (2), FLOWSHEET

novice division
Definition: A group of inexperienced, beginning debaters who compete against each other at a debate tournament. Novice division is usually debaters who have never debated before and have very few trophies.
Synonym: BEGINNER'S DIVISION
See also: DIVISION, TOURNAMENT

O

objection

Definition: An argument against a plan, value, or another argument.

Example: An *objection* to the argument that space development helps only the rich might be "Space development has helped Third World countries by giving satellite information that helps farming and business."

See also: DISADVANTAGE, RESPONSE, SOLVENCY, VALUE OBJECTION, WORKABILITY

objective

See: GOAL

observation

Definition: A general argument that indirectly responds to a case, plan, value, or argument; an argument statement that is further supported.

Example: "Observation: There is a need for home health care." "Observation: The affirmative case is not topical." "Observation: The present system is very good."

See also: CONTENTION, OVERVIEW, TOPICALITY, UNDERVIEW

offcase

Definition: Arguments made against the general idea of the affirmative case, against the affirmative plan, or against the value example, and not the specific affirmative case arguments. Value objections, countervalues, disadvantages, workability arguments, and topicality arguments are typical offcase arguments.

See also: CASESIDE, PLANSIDE

off-topic debate

Definition: A type of college debate in which humor, wit, and extemporaneous research and analysis are emphasized.

See also: CEDA DEBATE, DEBATE FORMATS, NDT DEBATE

omit

Definition: To exclude; to leave out.

Example: A debater might *omit* an argument by forgetting to read a page in her first affirmative speech.

See also: DROP, IGNORE

on

Definition: To be addressing a specific issue or argument.

Usage: I am on the B point, the use of fireworks. *(I am now dealing with the arguments about the use of fireworks that are organized as the B point.)*

See also: CLASH, FOUR-STEP REFUTATION

on balance

See: NET

one-minute rule

Definition: A rule giving each speaker one minute before his or her speech to prepare. After each speech or cross-examination period, the upcoming speaker may take up to one minute of time to prepare for his or her speech. The speaker must begin speaking after the one minute is up. Varying versions of the one-minute rule give two, three, or even four minutes before each speech.

See also: PREPARATION TIME

one-person debate

Definition: One debater argues for the resolution, and one other debater argues against it. Lincoln-Douglas debate uses a one-person debate format.

Synonym: TWO-SPEAKER DEBATE

See also: LINCOLN-DOUGLAS DEBATE, TEAM DEBATE

open division

Definition: A group of debate teams that compete against each other at a tournament. At some tournaments just experienced teams debate in open division. At other tournaments all debate teams compete in an open division.

See also: DIVISION, TOURNAMENT

operational definition

Definition: To define a term or terms in the resolution implicitly within the case, usually by the arguments presented in a case.

Example: A team that advocated fusion nuclear energy to support the resolution "RESOLVED: That nuclear power should be encouraged" *operationally defines* the phrase "nuclear power" to mean "fusion nuclear energy" with the arguments in their case.

Usage: All terms will be operationally defined. *(The words in the resolution will be defined by the affirmative case.)*

See also: TOPICALITY

opinion

Definition: A belief that can be objectively proven or disproven.

Example: "We have sold arms to the Contras" is an objectively true statement. "Selling arms to the Contras is good" is an *opinion* because it is a belief, not a statement of what is known as a fact to be true.

See also: BELIEF, FACT, VALUE

opposition

Definition: The team that one debates against. The affirmative's opposition is the negative. The negative's opposition is the affirmative.

Usage: They're stiff opposition. *(That team is a tough team to debate.)*

See also: AFFIRMATIVE, COMPETITION, NEGATIVE

oral critique

Definition: Occurs when a judge gives comments to debaters at the end of or during a debate. An oral critique includes a judge's comments about what the debaters did well, what they need to improve on, and perhaps some insight on the issues raised in the debate.

See also: JUDGE, ORAL DECISION

oral decision

Definition: Occurs when a judge states out loud who won the debate and why. Many tournaments ask judges not to give *oral decisions.*

See also: JUDGE, ORAL CRITIQUE

oratory

Definition: A speaking event in which a speaker attempts to persuade the audience to change their beliefs or their actions.

Synonym: PERSUASION

Oregon style debate

Definition: Debate format between two teams. The debaters present their cases, question each other, and then give rebuttal speeches.

See also: DEBATE FORMATS

organization

Definition: The ordering and structuring of arguments.

Example: Usually cases are *organized* using outline *organization:*

I. Railroad track crossings are dangerous.
   A. Many crossings are not clearly marked.
   B. Thousands of railroad-crossing deaths and injuries occur each year.

Responses to opponent arguments are usually *organized* and presented in numerical order:

1. Crossings are clearly marked.
2. Markings are improving.
3. Crossing markers save lives.

See also: OUTLINE ORGANIZATION

orthodox debate

See: OXFORD STYLE DEBATE

ought-is fallacy

See: IS-OUGHT FALLACY

out (1)

Definition: To make the elimination rounds.

Usage: Did you make it out? *(Do you have a good enough record to make it to the finals rounds?)*

Note: Confusion may occur between Out (1) and Out (2). Ask for a clarification.

See also: IN, OUT (2)

out (2)

Definition: To no longer be in competition at a tournament.

Usage: Are you out? *(Are you no longer competing in the tournament because you did not have a good enough record or because you lost a finals round and were eliminated?)*

Note: Confusion may occur between Out (2) and Out (1). Ask for clarification.

See also: IN, OUT (1)

outline

Definition: An organized and structured series of argument claims, usually without support.

Example: I. Nerve gas production is disastrous.

    A. Nerve gas increases the risk of war.

    B. Nerve gas endangers the environment.

    C. Nerve gas production harms wildlife.

See also: ORGANIZATION, OUTLINE ORGANIZATION

outline organization

Definition: The structuring and ordering of arguments using three rules: 1) Main arguments are supported by indented lower arguments; 2) Numbers or letters are attached to the arguments to indicate their order, including, in this order:

I.

  A.

    1.

     a.

      1)

       a);

3) A lower argument must have a partner. A "1." must have a "2."; an "a)" must have a "b)."

Example: I. Economic growth is bad.

  A. Economic growth increases pollution.

    1. Economic growth creates air pollution.

    2. Economic growth creates terrible water pollution.

     a. Economic growth leads to dumping of pollutants into water.

     b. Water pollution is dangerous to people's health.

     c. Water pollution endangers important species.

  B. Economic growth leads to heightened expectations that turn false when the economy falters.

  C. Economic growth increases the risk of war.

    1. Growth usually leaves money for military buildup.

    2. Growth leads to nationalistic pride that turns militaristic.

    3. Militarism leads to increased risk of war.

Notice the indenting of lower points. Notice that lower points support the main points they fall under. Notice that each point is given a number or letter and that there is no "A." without at least a "B.", no "1." without at least a "2.", and no "a." without at least a "b."

See also: ORGANIZATION, OUTLINE

out rounds

See: ELIMINATION ROUNDS

outweigh

Definition: To be more important than.

Usage: This nuclear war disadvantage outweighs their 0.1 percent inflation advantage. *(In comparison, the nuclear war disadvantage is more important than the inflation advantage.)*

See also: COMPARISON, SYSTEMS ANALYSIS, WEIGH

oversimplification

Definition: To make an argument so uncomplex as to be inaccurate.

Example: To describe the situation in El Salvador as "It is either the good guys or the bad guys" is an *oversimplification.*

See also: FALLACY, RED HERRING

overview

Definition: An observation, or general argument, made prior to a series of arguments.

Usage: On the disadvantages, I want to make an overview: None of them show the plan would be more harmful than its advantage. *(Before I make specific responses, I want to make the argument that the disadvantages do not outweigh the advantage of the affirmative plan.)*

See also: CONTENTION, OBSERVATION, UNDERVIEW

Oxford style debate

Definition: A debate format between two teams. There are four speeches and two rebuttals and no cross-examination.

See also: DEBATE FORMATS

P

PMA/PMG/PMN

See: PLAN MEET ADVANTAGE/GOAL/NEED

pairing

See: MATCHING

paradigm

Definition: A view of how a debate should be judged. There are many *paradigms.* A judge might weigh the advantages versus disadvantages; decide if the affirmative has proven the resolution adequately; look to see which team has the better skills; or look to see if the affirmative has won all five stock issues.

Usage: What is your paradigm? *(How do you judge debates?* or *What arguments or skills do you like to see in a debate?)*

See also: CRITIC OF ARGUMENT, HYPOTHESIS TESTING, JUDICIAL PARADIGM, NARRATIVE PARADIGM, POLICY SYSTEMS, SKILLS JUDGE, STOCK ISSUES PARADIGM, SYSTEMS ANALYSIS, TABULA RASA, VALUE

paradox

Definition: An apparent contradiction or absurd argument that may in fact be true.

Example: "There is one rule about debate: There are no rules."
See also: CONTRADICTION

paragraph case

Definition: A case structure that supports its claims with two or more pieces of evidence.
Example: A *paragraph case* might include an advantage like this:
I. Bottle refund will help clean the environment.
    A. Most states do not have refundable bottles. (Followed by four pieces of evidence.)
    B. Nonrefundable bottles encourage litter. (Followed by six pieces of evidence.)
    C. Litter seriously damages the environment. (Followed by seven pieces of evidence.)
    D. Refundable bottles would decrease litter and help the environment. (Followed by five pieces of evidence.)
See also: CASE STRUCTURES, OUTLINE ORGANIZATION

parallel arguments

Definition: Arguments that are independent of each other.
Example: Three *parallel arguments* might be "Cars create pollution," "Cars create traffic messes," and "Cars are involved in accidents." They are *parallel* because they do not depend upon one another to be true. The arguments "Cars create pollution," and "Car pollution kills many people" would not be *parallel arguments* because the second argument depends on the first—car pollution kills many people only if, as the first argument demonstrates, cars really do pollute. These dependent arguments are called "serial arguments."
Antonym: SERIAL ARGUMENTS
See also: CAUSAL LINK, ORGANIZATION, REASONING

parameters

Definition: Used in conjunction with the NDT resolution to help define the meaning of the terms in the resolution.
Example: For the topic "RESOLVED: That the United States should significantly alter its trade policies with South American countries," the *parameters* might include the following: "Alter its trade policies" shall mean "to change fundamental aspects of U.S. trade policies, including mili-

tary and commercial sales, and shall not include political actions or diplomacy"; "South America" shall mean "those countries to the south of Panama, north of the Drake Passage, east of Galapagos Island, and west of Trinidad."

See also: PROBLEM AREA, RESOLUTION, TOPICALITY

parliamentary debate
See: BRITISH FORMAT DEBATE

particular audience
Definition: The audience that is specifically addressed. Debaters try to convince a *particular audience,* the judge in front of them—not all the judges in the country.
See also: UNIVERSAL AUDIENCE

partner
Definition: The person one debates with on a debate team.
Example: Tyrone and Sadi are *partners* because they debate together.
See also: TEAM, TEAM DEBATE

pathos
Definition: Persuasiveness; emotional appeals.
Example: "Please, save the lives of those being tortured in prison cells in Chile. The cells are in terrible condition, and prisoners are humiliated by the guards."
See also: ETHOS, LOGOS

perception
Definition: The views or beliefs of people.
Usage: Even though an arms cutoff to El Salvador may not actually lead to communist attacks, the right wing there will *perceive* that the cutoffs will lead to attacks and stage a bloody coup. *(Even though cutting arms sales to El Salvador may not actually cause communist attacks, right-wing death squads there may believe they will, and these death squads will then violently attempt to take over the country.)*
See also: BELIEF, DISADVANTAGE

periodicals

Definition: Magazines, journals, and newsletters.

Example: Newsweek, Journal of the American Medical Association, Kiplinger report

See also: BOOK, RESEARCH

peripheral argument

Definition: An argument that is not directly related to the main topic.

Example: On a drug testing topic, some teams made *peripheral arguments* about genetic screening of workers. Genetic screening doesn't sound directly related to drug testing, but, in fact, several experts felt that drug testing would lead to genetic screening.

See also: DIVERSIONARY PROOFS, SQUIRREL CASE

permanence

Definition: The expectation that a policy will remain the same for a long period of time.

Example: A negative team may argue that the affirmative plan is not needed because the new administration will change the present system. The affirmative then could show *permanence* by arguing that the new administration will not change the present system.

Usage: Make the affirmative prove permanence. *(Make our opponents show that the current policy will remain the same for a long period of time.)*

See also: INCREMENTALISM, INHERENCY

permutation

Definition: To argue that major elements of a counterplan could be implemented with the affirmative plan, and therefore those elements of the counterplan are not relevant to the debate; to argue that the major elements of a value alternative could be supported with the value object, and therefore those elements of the value alternative are not relevant to the debate.

Example: A plan might be to ban polygraphs in courtrooms. The counterplan might be to use polygraphs in courtrooms and ban polygraphs outside of the court. The counterplan could be *permuted* by excluding the portion that bans polygraphs outside the court because that could happen at the same time the plan banned polygraphs in courtrooms. The *permutation* would make any advantage stemming from banning polygraphs outside of courtrooms irrelevant.

See also: CAPTURE, COMPETITION, COUNTERPLAN, EXTRA-COMPETITIVENESS, VALUE ALTERNATIVE

persuasion

Definition: To get other people to agree to new beliefs or to do something new; a speech in which the audience is urged to agree to a new belief or to do something new (oratory).

Example: A debater tries to *persuade* her judge to agree that democracy is the most important value. A debater tries to *persuade* his judge to vote for the Equal Rights Amendment by making strong arguments for it.

See also: ORATORY, PATHOS

philosophical competitiveness

Definition: The issue of whether the counterplan and plan, or the value alternative and value example, are theoretically incompatible.

Example: An affirmative offers a value alternative to supervise suspect employees, instead of using random drug testing, the value object. The affirmative could argue supervision is *philosophically competitive* with random drug testing because supervision of suspect employees promotes the theory of innocent until proven guilty, while random drug testing promotes the philosophy of guilty until proven innocent.

See also: COMPETITIVENESS, COUNTERPLAN, VALUE ALTERNATIVE

philosophy

Definition: The position that a team supports in a debate.

Usage: The negative *philosophy* in today's debate is that current malpractice insurance is adequate. *(The negative will support current malpractice insurance.)*

See also: POSITION

Pi Kappa Delta

Definition: A college speech and debate organization that promotes the art of persuasion through forensic contests and seminars.

See also: DELTA SIGMA RHO-TAU KAPPA ALPHA (DSR–TKA)

pick up (1)

Definition: (n.) An argument that is presented in the first negative speech and then, usually, is rebuilt in the second negative constructive. (v.) The act of rebuilding an argument presented in the first negative speech.

Example: The first negative speaker argues that a direct elections plan will cause dangerous neo-Nazi candidates to win elections. The second negative speaker then rebuilds this argument in her speech. The neo-Nazi candidate argument would therefore be called a *pick up* and the second negative would *pick up* this argument.

See also: DISADVANTAGE, DROP

pick up (2)

Definition: To win a debate round.

Usage: Did we pick up the last round? *(Did we win the last debate round?)*

See also: LOSE, ORAL DECISION, WIN

plan

Definition: The affirmative's suggestion that a course of action be taken that supports the resolution; inherent change.

Example: A *plan* might be to build new freeways throughout the country. A *plan* might be to ban the Strategic Defense Initiative ("Star Wars").

Usage: The plan is not topical. *(The plan does not follow nor support the resolution as it should.)* What is your plan? *(What action does your plan support?)*

See also: CASE, FIAT, INHERENT CHANGE, PLANSIDE, STATUS QUO, TOPICALITY

plan meet need/advantage/goal

Definition: A solvency argument that shows the affirmative plan will not meet the need or will not achieve the advantage or goal.

Usage: I will argue a plan meet need: The use of colored thread paper money will not prevent counterfeiting. *(I will argue that the plan will not solve the counterfeiting problem.)* PMA: Using coal scrubbers will not reduce acid rain. *(The plan's use of scrubbers will not reduce acid rain.)*

Note: Frequently abbreviated PMN, PMA, and PMG.

Synonym: SOLVENCY ARGUMENTS

See also: SOLVENCY, WORKABILITY

plan objection

Definition: A solvency argument, a workability argument, or a disadvantage against a plan.

Example: *Plan objection:* The affirmative plan to encourage geothermal power will create pollution.

See also: DISADVANTAGE, SOLVENCY, WORKABILITY

plank

Definition: A part of a plan. There are usually five planks in a plan, including: a board, mandates, funding, enforcement, and intent.

Example: Plan One: The affirmative will establish a seven-member, self-perpetuating board given all minimally necessary staff, funding, and facilities to ensure that the affirmative mandates are effectively implemented.

Usage: What is in your plank two? *(What is included in the second part of your plan?)*

Synonym: SECTION

See also: BOARD, ENFORCEMENT, FUNDING, INTENT, MANDATES, PLAN

planside

Definition: The arguments in the debate that respond to or support the negative arguments made against the affirmative plan; the arguments that do not directly respond to or support the arguments advanced by the affirmative case. The disadvantage and workability arguments, as well as the solvency arguments that were not made directly against an affirmative case argument, are *planside* issues.

Usage: Go to planside. *(In your notes of the debate, direct your attention to the issues the negative presented in their attacks on the plan, usually second negative arguments.*) We outweigh planside. (*Our arguments supporting our plan are more important than the negative's arguments against the plan, and we should, therefore, win the debate.*)

See also: CASESIDE, OFFCASE, PLAN

planside barrier
Definition: An inherency standard that shows that the present system is different from the affirmative plan.
Example: The *planside barrier* to a national health insurance program might be the present system's reliance on private insurance companies to provide insurance instead of having the government provide the insurance.
Usage: What's your planside barrier? (*What is different about your plan from the present system?*)
Note: "Planside barrier" is often mistakenly taken to mean "something that prevents the present system from adopting the affirmative plan" (*see* SHOULD-COULD FALLACY).
See also: CASESIDE BARRIER, INHERENCY, INHERENT BARRIER

plausibility
Definition: The believability of an argument because of the strength of the rationale for that argument.
Example: The *plausibility* that drug testing will cause nuclear war is very low because it seems unlikely that drug testing would cause nuclear war.
Usage: The argument showing that recycling centers will solve garbage problems seems plausible. (*The "recycling centers" argument seems believable because it sounds reasonable.*)
See also: DOUBT, PROBABILITY, RISK

point
Definition: The main idea of an argument.
Example: The main *point* of the argument "I will stress the different ways nuclear power plants harm plantlife and endanger water supplies and the air" is that nuclear power plants hurt the environment.
Usage: What's the point of that argument? (*What is the main idea of that argument?*)
See also: ARGUMENT, CLAIM

policy

Definition: A course of action.
Example: Jimmy Carter had a *policy* of promoting human rights. Ronald Reagan had a *policy* of decreasing taxes. Affirmative teams (in policy debate) support new *policies* with their plans; for example, increasing support services for the abused. Negatives support the *policy* of the present system—current support services—or a counterplan *policy*—banning all support services.
See also: PLAN, RESOLUTION OF POLICY

policy debate

Definition: Debate using a policy topic, including high school policy debate and college NDT debate.
See also: HIGH SCHOOL POLICY DEBATE, NDT DEBATE, NONPOLICY DEBATE, RESOLUTION OF POLICY, RESOLUTION OF QUASI-POLICY

policy systems

Definition: The comparison of policies and their effects to determine the best policy. A person who uses a *policy systems* approach to a debate would examine the policies supported by the affirmative and negative, the risks of each policy, and the advantages and disadvantages of each policy. The policy with the greatest advantages would be considered the best policy.
See also: PARADIGM, SYSTEMS ANALYSIS, VALUE

policymaker

Definition: A judge who uses policy systems analysis to come to decisions; a judge who views the debate as a legislative session.
See also: LEGISLATIVE DEBATE, POLICY SYSTEMS, SYSTEMS ANALYSIS

popular appeal

Definition: To make an argument that is supported by most people.
Example: To argue for the death penalty in the United States would be a *popular appeal* since most Americans favor the death penalty. Arguments against drug use probably also have *popular appeal*.
See also: BANDWAGON FALLACY, PATHOS

Portland style debate

Definition: A debate in which 1) background information on the topic is provided; 2) different speakers present proposals and ideas about the topic; 3) the audience asks the speakers questions about their proposals; and 4) the speakers compare each other's arguments and proposals.

Synonym: SYMPOSIUM STYLE DEBATE

See also: DEBATE FORMATS

position

Definition: A stand on an issue that a debater supports.

Usage: Our position in this debate will be that because the electoral college violates the principle of one person one vote, we need to move to direct elections. *(The stand that we will support in this debate is that direct elections are superior to the electoral college because they better insure the principle of one person one vote.)*

Synonym: PHILOSOPHY

See also: SYSTEMS ANALYSIS

post hoc fallacy

Definition: An argument that says one event causes another because the two events occurred at about the same time.

Example: "The school bell causes buses to arrive because at the same time the bell rings at school, the buses arrive to take students home." "The economy declined while Jimmy Carter was in office, so Carter caused the economy to decline."

See also: ASSOCIATION, CAUSAL LINK, FALLACY

power matching

Definition: To make debate teams with similar win-loss records in a tournament compete against each other.

Example: After two or three rounds of debate, tournaments usually begin *power matching*. Teams with 3–0 records hit other 3–0 teams, while teams with 2–1 records are scheduled to debate other 2–1 teams.

Synonym: POWER PAIRING

See also: HIGH-HIGH, HIGH-LOW, MISMATCHING

power pairing
See: POWER MATCHING

power protect
See: MISMATCH

preempt
See: PREEMPTION

preemption
Definition: To respond to an argument before that argument has been made.
Example: A negative team argues that the affirmative plan will cause a large deficit. The negative predicts that the affirmative will respond to this deficit argument by suggesting that the plan's cigarette tax will pay for the plan and, therefore, prevent any deficit. So, the negative *preempts* this cigarette argument by making the argument "Cigarette taxes will bring in very little money" before the affirmative even has a chance to say that the cigarette tax will bring in enough money.
Usage: Preempt. Don't let them argue that negotiations will stop the war. *(I am going to show you why any argument from my opponent that shows that negotiations will stop the war will not be a good argument.)*
See also: CLASH, REFUTATION

preliminary round
Definition: A debate prior to the final rounds in a tournament. At most tournaments there are five to eight preliminary rounds of debate. The teams with the best win-loss records at the end of the preliminary rounds advance to the final rounds.
Usage: How'd you do in prelims? *(How did you do in the rounds prior to the final rounds in the tournament?)*
See also: ELIMINATION ROUNDS

premise
Definition: The underlying assumption of an argument.

Example: The *premise* of Marcie's charge that Don was stealing money was that she knew $400 disappeared while Don was in charge of the money box. One *premise* of a case to give food aid to starving Africans is that people there need that food to eat.

See also: ARGUMENT, ENTHYMEME, MAJOR PREMISE, MINOR PREMISE, SYLLOGISM

prep
See: PREPARATION

prep time
See: PREPARATION TIME

preparation
Definition: To get ready to debate or speak.

Usage: We need to prep up against the Thailand case. *(We need to get ready for our debate against the Thailand case by researching and planning arguments.)*

See also: RESEARCH

preparation time
Definition: The time given during a debate to prepare to speak. Tournaments often give each team a total of four to ten minutes of preparation time that can be used whenever a team wants. For example, if there are six minutes of preparation time and a second affirmative speaker takes two minutes of preparation time before she speaks, that would leave four minutes for preparation before the first affirmative and second affirmative rebuttals. At other tournaments, each speaker receives one to four minutes preparation time before each speech.

Usage: How much prep time do we have left? *(How much of our total preparation time do we have left to take?)* What's the preparation time at this tournament? *(How much time is given to each team during a debate for preparation?)*

Synonym: DOWNTIME

See also: ONE-MINUTE RULE

present system
See:　STATUS QUO

preset match
Definition:　To schedule teams to debate each other prior to the beginning of the tournament. At most tournaments, the first two or three debate rounds are scheduled in preset matches before the tournament begins. Teams are usually *preset matched* against other teams randomly, or against teams that are not in the same district.
Usage:　Are these rounds preset? *(Were these debates scheduled prior to the beginning of the tournament?)*
See also:　MATCHING, POWER MATCHING

press
Definition:　To point out a flaw in the opponent's argument or arguments.
Example:　A *press* against the argument "All stores overcharge their customers because one store in one city overcharged its customers" is "The argument is flawed because one store is an isolated example and does not prove that all stores overcharge."
Usage:　Press their case. *(Point out the flaws in their case.)* All you did was press. You never read any evidence. *(All you did was point out flaws in their arguments; you never countered their arguments with any evidence.)*
See also:　CLASH, REFUTATION

presumption
Definition:　The initial beliefs of the judge or audience about the resolution and the argument claims advanced by debaters. Presumption determines who must prove their case and may decide which team wins if the debate ends in a tie. Here are four views of presumption. First, traditional presumption is with the present system. Often referred to as "the status quo is innocent until proven guilty," it generally means that any change must be justified. In policy debate, this almost always means that the negative is given presumption.

　　Second, risk presumption is against the risk of uncertainty. The larger a policy or value change is and the riskier a value or policy is, the greater the presumption is against that value or policy. Risk presumption can be for or against the affirmative, depending on the risk of uncertainty and the amount of change advocated.

Third, hypothesis-testing presumption is against the resolution or a claim. Debaters must prove any claim they make, and the affirmative must prove the resolution. Hypothesis-testing presumption is, therefore, always for the negative.

Fourth, psychological presumption is with the judge's or audience's beliefs. If the judge agrees with the resolution or the affirmative's proposal, then presumption is with the affirmative. If the judge is against the resolution or the affirmative's proposal, then presumption is with the negative.

Usage: I voted on presumption. *(I felt the round was essentially a tie and I therefore voted for the team that I gave presumption; or I felt one of the teams failed to support what they needed to in order to win. So, I voted for the other team, the team that I gave presumption.)*

See also: BURDEN OF PROOF

prima facie

Definition: To make a convincing case when first presented. Most judges require the affirmative to make a *prima facie* case. For some judges, this means (in policy debate) proving significance, inherency, and solvency, or (in value debate) establishing a criterion and proving the criterion is met in the case. For other judges, it means giving a good reason for the plan (policy debate) or the case (value debate).

Usage: The affirmative case was not prima facie. *(The affirmative case failed to make a convincing case for the judge.)*

See also: BURDEN OF PROOF, PRESUMPTION

primary research

Definition: Research directly from books, magazines, newspapers, or documents, but not handbooks, for evidence and information on the resolution.

Example: Joe engages in *primary research* when he goes to the library to find evidence. He does not engage in *primary research* when he gets evidence from teammates or handbooks.

See also: EVIDENCE, HANDBOOKS

primary source

Definition: A directly quoted expert.

Example: Henry Kissinger would be a *primary source* about foreign policy since he works in that field. A newspaper editorial would not be a *primary source* since it will rely on secondhand information from others to make its opinion.

See also: HEARSAY EVIDENCE, SECONDARY SOURCE

pro and con

Definition: For and against; affirmative and negative.

Example: Fernando presents the *pro* arguments for the use of chemical weapons. John presents the *con* arguments against the use of chemical weapons.

Usage: Give me the pros and cons of the busing issue. *(Give arguments for and against busing.)*

See also: AFFIRMATIVE, NEGATIVE

probability

Definition: The chance that an event will occur.

Example: The *probability* that someone hiccuping will cause nuclear war is low; the *probability* that the spread of nuclear weapons to new countries will cause nuclear war is much higher.

See also: PLAUSIBILITY, RISK

problem

Definition: An undesirable situation.

Example: A *problem* might be increased poverty. Economic growth is usually considered good, but for those arguing that it hurts the environment, it might be considered a *problem*.

See also: HARMS, NEED, SIGNIFICANCE

problem area

Definition: The main issue; the main problem that the resolution attempts to address.

Example: The 1988–1989 problem area for the high school policy topic was "What should the federal government do to enhance the quality of life for U.S. citizens over 65?"

See also: PARAMETERS, RESOLUTION

problem-solving debate
See: WASHINGTON STYLE DEBATE

process
Definition: A way to do something; a procedure; an administrative action or way of acting.
Example: A *process* might be how the FDA permits drugs to be marketed, or the way that courts accept appeals.
See also: PROCESS ADVANTAGE

process advantage
Definition: A plan's administrative benefit; an argument that shows the plan will do something in a better way.
Example: A plan might reorganize AIDS research efforts to make the research more efficient. The plan might gain a *process advantage* of increased efficiency. A plan to reorganize Social Security might gain the *process advantage* of preventing computer foulups and interdepartmental confusion.
See also: ADVANTAGE, PROCESS COUNTERPLAN, PROCESS DISADVANTAGE

process counterplan
Definition: A counterplan that implements the affirmative plan through a different process.
Example: A matrix counterplan puts the affirmative plan into a computer and waits for the results of the computer to tell how to best implement the plan. A states counterplan implements the affirmative counterplan through state governments instead of the federal government. There are many other *process counterplans*: the referendum counterplan puts the affirmative up to a popular vote; the study counterplan studies the plan and its advantage prior to implementing the plan; the mediation counterplan seeks to get both sides in a dispute to work out their problems.
See also: AGENT COUNTERPLAN, COMPETITIVENESS, COUNTERPLAN, EXCEPTIONS COUNTERPLANS, NON-TOPICAL

process disadvantage
Definition: A plan's administrative harm; an argument showing that the plan will do something in a worse way.

Example: "This plan to give more money to welfare recipients would create more bureaucracy."

See also: DISADVANTAGE, PROCESS ADVANTAGE

proof

Definition: To support an argument persuasively; to give an argument a solid rationale.

Example: A team might argue that the spread of nuclear weapons to new countries increases the risk of nuclear war. What would constitute *proof* for this argument? Perhaps evidence that shows new countries won't have safety systems for the new bombs and will thereby increase the risks of accidents and accidental war.

Usage: Where is the proof for your argument? *(Where is the persuasive support for your argument?)*

See also: BURDEN OF PROOF, EVIDENCE

propensity

Definition: The possibility that an event will occur.

Usage: The present system has a propensity to deal with the water shortage situation. *(The present system is likely to deal with the water shortage situation.)* What is the propensity for the status quo to do that? *(What is the likelihood that the status quo would do that?)*

See also: MECHANISM, MINOR REPAIR, MOTIVE, PLAUSIBILITY, PROBABILITY

proposal

See: PLAN

proposition

See: RESOLUTION

proposition of fact, policy, quasi-policy, and value

See: RESOLUTION OF FACT, RESOLUTION OF POLICY, RESOLUTION OF QUASI-POLICY, RESOLUTION OF VALUE

Protagaras

Definition: Ancient Greek scholar who is considered the orginator of debate.

public debate

Definition: A debate for the public.

Example: The presidential debates between Reagan and Mondale were *public debates.* Academic debaters who compete in front of the public—for example, in front of the Rotary Club—are engaged in *public debate.*

See also: ACADEMIC DEBATE, DEBATE, LAY JUDGE

public speaking

Definition: Speaking in front of an audience.

Example: When Michael Dukakis, George Bush, Jesse Jackson, and Bob Dole spoke to crowds during their presidential campaigns, they were engaged in *public speaking.* When debaters debate in front of their judge, they are engaged in *public speaking.* When people speak to each other in a conversation, that usually is not considered *public speaking.*

See also: DELIVERY, SPEAKER

public speaking paradigm

See: SKILLS PARADIGM

pull

Definition: To restate the importance of a previously made argument.

Usage: Pull the B subpoint where we argued that alcohol sales are increasing. *(We remind you of the importance of the "alcohol sales are increasing" argument we made previously in our B subpoint.)*

Synonym: PULL ACROSS

See also: EXTEND, REBUTTAL

pull across

See: PULL

quadratic relationship

Definition: An increase or decrease in one event causes or is associated with proportionally small, then large, then huge amounts of another event.

Example: There is probably a *quadratic relationship* between radiation and cancer. In small doses, radiation causes very little increase in the risk of cancer. In slightly greater doses, radiation causes a large increase in the risk of cancer. In very large doses, the risk of cancer dramatically increases. The relationship between street lamps and accidents would be *quadratic* if one street lamp on a road reduced one accident per year, two street lamps reduced accidents by four, and three street lamps reduced accidents by twelve.

See also: LINEAR

qualifier

Definition: The strength of an argument.

Example: If we say that drugs are bad because studies on animals show they are, we might place a *qualifier* in the argument; for example, we might say that drugs are "probably" bad.

See also: RESERVATION, TOULMIN MODEL OF ARGUMENT

qualitative harms

Definition: Undesirable effects upon a cherished value.

Example: A *qualitative harm* might be that bail violates the value of believing a person is innocent before proven guilty. Typical *qualitative harms* include harms to justice, to democracy, to freedom, and to social justice.

See also: HARMS, QUANTITATIVE HARMS

quandary

Definition: A state of being in which one is unable to respond to a question or argument because of uncertainty; to be in a dilemma.

Example: Sarah was in a *quandary* because she couldn't decide whether to answer the question "yes" or "no"—either way she would be in trouble.

See also: CONTRADICTION, DILEMMA

quantitative harms

Definition: Undesirable results that are measured numerically.

Example: "Thirty thousand deaths occur each year" is a *quantitative harm*. "Forty-four percent of farms are going bankrupt" is a *quantitative harm*.

See also: HARMS, QUALITATIVE HARMS

quasi-policy proposition/resolution

See: RESOLUTION OF QUASI-POLICY

question

Definition: To ask for an answer to a query.

Example: "How many people in Taiwan want to be allied with the United States?" is a *question* because it directly asks for an answer.

See also: CROSS-EXAMINATION

question begging

Definition: To not answer, or avoid, a question.

Example: To the question "How will you stop the use of drugs?" an answer that *question begs* might be "Well, drugs are a serious problem. They need to be stopped."

See also: BEGGING THE QUESTION, CROSS-EXAMINATION, RESPONDENT

questioner

Definition: The person who asks questions. In cross-examination, one person is designated as the questioner and asks the previous speaker questions.

See also: CROSS-EXAMINATION, RESPONDENT

quick

Definition: To speak or think rapidly.

Usage: They're quick. *(They speak or think rapidly.)* She's really quick in the 1AR. *(She speaks rapidly in her first affirmative rebuttal speech.)*

See also: COMMUNICATION, DELIVERY

quotes

See: EVIDENCE

R

rank

Definition: A judge's ordering, from best to worst, of speakers in a debate or speaking event. Judges *rank* the debater they felt was best in a debate as number 1. The next best debater is *ranked* 2. The next, 3, and the last, 4. Ties in *rank* are usually not permitted.

Usage: Average rank was 2.12. *(A speaker received a 2.12 based on the average of ranks received in debates at a tournament.)*

See also: RATING, SPEAKER AWARDS, SPEAKER POINTS

rating

Definition: A numerical score that reflects how well the judge felt a debater did in a debate. A judge *rates* a debater according to a scale given on the ballot for the debate. For example, the ballot may have the following *rating* scale: 1: unprepared; 2: fair; 3: average; 4: good; 5: excellent. If a debater did a fair job of analyzing, the judge might give a 2. If a debater did a great job of delivering, the judge would give a 4 or 5. There are usually a total of thirty rating points a debater may receive.

See also: SPEAKER AWARDS, SPEAKER POINTS

rationale

Definition: To give a reason for; to provide support for an argument.

See: EVIDENCE

reason for decision

Definition: A statement explaining why one voted for a certain team.

Example: "I voted for the negative because of the disadvantage and the reduction in affirmative significance. I was convinced the plan to increase jails would greatly damage the economy because of its high taxes. The negative also showed that there are not that many criminals let free, nor are there serious problems in the jail."

Usage: What was the reason for decision? *(Why did the judge vote the way he or she did?)*

See also: BALLOT, DECISION, PARADIGM

reasonable standard

Definition: A topicality standard that argues a meaningful definition should be accepted, even if that definition is unusual and even if there is another, "better," definition.

Example: On a resolution "RESOLVED: That the United States should expand its space policy," a *reasonable definition* of "space" might be "an open area," even though many might think it is best defined as "outer space."

See also: BEST DEFINITION, RESOLUTION, TOPICALITY

reasoning

Definition: The process of connecting ideas and events. Five main types of reasoning are causal, sign, analogy, generalization, and specialization (classification).

Example: *Reasoning* a connection between a raised bridge and traffic backups, a speaker might argue, "A raised bridge creates traffic backups." One might *reason* that a large room with many books neatly arranged in rows with Library of Congress numbers is a library. *Reasoning* in debate might be analyzing whether a generic disadvantage applies to a specific affirmative plan.

Usage: On a ballot, judges are asked to rate debaters' reasoning. *(The judge should give a rating number indicating the quality of the debater's connections between ideas and arguments and issues in the debate.)*

See also: ANALOGY, CAUSAL, CLASSIFICATION, FALLACY, GENER-
ALIZATION, SIGN REASONING, SPECIALIZATION

rebuild
Definition: To engage in rebuttal.
See: REBUTTAL (2)

rebuttal (1)
Definition: A speech in the latter portion of a debate. In team debate there are four rebuttals: the first negative rebuttal, the first affirmative rebuttal, the second negative rebuttal, the second affirmative rebuttal. In Lincoln-Douglas debate there are two rebuttals: the affirmative rebuttal and the negative rebuttal.
Usage: You had a really good rebuttal. *(You did very well in the speech you gave in the latter portion of a debate.)*
See also: FIRST AFFIRMATIVE REBUTTAL, FIRST NEGATIVE RE-
BUTTAL, REBUTTAL (2), SECOND AFFIRMATIVE REBUT-
TAL, SECOND NEGATIVE REBUTTAL

rebuttal (2)
Definition: To engage in a process of re-explaining one's previous argument, responding to opponent arguments, extending with new insights on the original argument, and crystallizing the issue by explaining how the arguments show that one has won the debate.
Example: "We originally argued that current highways are dangerous because of the lack of shoulders and poor paving. Our opponent had one response: that there were not that many deaths on the roads. First, there are still many injuries. Second, deaths are significant on the roads, according to the Highway Transportation Committee. I'd extend by arguing that highways will continue to deteriorate and that there will be a dramatic increase in highway deaths. (Debater reads evidence.) So, overall it should be clear that highways are dangerous, and that is why the affirmative plan for new and safe highway construction should be encouraged."

See also: CLASH, EXTENSION, FOUR-STEP REFUTATION, REBUT-
TAL (1), REFUTATION

receiver

Definition: A person who listens to, interprets, and comes to an understanding of what another person is saying. A judge is a receiver because he or she listens to, interprets, and comes to
an understanding of the debaters' arguments.

See also: AUDIENCE, JUDGE

red herring

Definition: An irrelevant argument raised to make it sound like the
other team supports something bad.

Example: A *red herring* argument against a jobs program is "The affirmative is supporting communism throughout the world
with its jobs and equality for everyone." This argument is a
red herring because communism is not relevant to a jobs program. Support for a jobs program does not mean support
for communism.

Usage: That argument is a red herring. *(That argument is irrelevant
and does not apply to our case.)*

See also: FALLACY

reductio ad absurdem

Definition: To take an argument to its extreme conclusion to point out
its limits or flaws.

Example: "If you are for the use of the military to deal with drug traf-
ficking, then you should also be for the military to deal with
other crimes, say, murder and rape. And at that point, you
will have the military in control of enforcing the law, and
the military will then obviously have too much power."

See also: FALLACY

redundancy

Definition: The issue of whether a counterplan and plan, or value alternative and value object, do essentially the same thing or
have the same effect. If they do, then the counterplan or
value alternative may be rejected.

Example: A debater might argue, "If the counterplan has the states
give people health insurance, this would be *redundant* with

the plan's use of the federal government to give people health insurance. Why do both?"

See also: ALTERNATIVES, COMPETITION, COUNTERPLAN

refutation

Definition: The process of exposing flaws in opponents' arguments.

Example: "Their evidence is out of date," "The source for their evidence is biased," and "Showing one city has dog problems does not prove the whole country has dog problems as the negative claims" are all examples of *refutation.*

See also: CLASH, COUNTERARGUMENT, FOUR-STEP REFUTATION, PRESS

relationship

Definition: A connection or association between two or more items or events.

Example: One might see a *relationship* between sexual activity and a disease and conclude that the disease is sexually transmitted.

See also: CAUSAL LINK, REASONING

relative

Definition: Dependent upon the situation.

Example: "I am for the legalization of drugs as long as drug use doesn't go way up" and "Early marriage is okay for some people but not for others" are both *relative* positions.

See also: ABSOLUTE

rep

See: REPUTATION

repair

See: MINOR REPAIR

repairs negative

Definition: A negative strategy that uses a minor repair.

See: MINOR REPAIR

repeat

Definition: An argument that is essentially the same as a previous argument.

Example: The arguments "Bureaucracy is rampant" and "Bureaucracy is widespread" *repeat* each other.

Usage: The first affirmative rebuttal needs to avoid repeating arguments. *(The speaker giving the first affirmative rebuttal speech needs to avoid giving the same argument more than once.)*

See also: CONCISE, GROUP, WORD ECONOMY

representative

Definition: To be a significant example of; to be typical of.

Example: If a resolution does not include the word "all"—for example, in the topic "RESOLVED: That guns should be banned"—some debate theorists have argued that the affirmative, while not needing to discuss all guns, does need to discuss a *representative* group of guns. So, one type of gun with very few sales and very little effect probably would not be *representative*. Handguns, however, might be *representative* because many are sold and they have a large impact.

Usage: The affirmative case is not representative. *(The affirmative is not discussing a typical example of the resolution and, therefore, should not be considered topical.)*

See also: COUNTERWARRANT, HASTY GENERALIZATION, TOPICALITY, TYPICALITY

reputation

Definition: A perception of a school, team, or debater.

Usage: They've got a really good rep. *(People perceive them to be really good.)*

See also: TEAM (1), TEAM (2)

research

Definition: To gather evidence from books, periodicals, documents, handbooks, and newspapers.

Usage: Let's do some research on this case. *(Let's get materials so we can find evidence for this case.)*

See also: EVIDENCE, PRIMARY RESEARCH

reservation

Definition: Exceptions to a proof given for a claim.

Example: A claim might be "Acid rain kills fish." A *reservation* to that claim might be "Acid rain kills fish except when the lake has naturally low acidity."

See also: QUALIFIER, TOULMIN MODEL OF ARGUMENT

resolution

Definition: The topic of debate; a stand on an issue that the affirmative supports and the negative rejects.

Example: A *resolution* might be "RESOLVED: That the United States should decriminalize marijuana." Another *resolution* might be "RESOLVED: That economic growth is more important than economic equality."

Usage: What is this year's resolution? *(Tell me what the topic of debate will be for this year's debates.)*

Synonyms: PROPOSITION, TOPIC

See also: RESOLUTION OF FACT, RESOLUTION OF POLICY, RESO-LUTION OF QUASI-POLICY, RESOLUTION OF VALUE, TOP-ICALITY

resolution of fact

Definition: A topic statement that makes an objective evaluation of an event, idea, person, place, or thing.

Example: "RESOLVED: That the temperature is 58 degrees" is a *resolution of fact* because it evaluates whether the temperature is 58 degrees. Since observations of a thermometer will tell us that it is or is not 58 degrees, the evaluation is objective.

See also: RESOLUTION, RESOLUTION OF POLICY, RESOLUTION OF QUASI-POLICY, RESOLUTION OF VALUE

resolution of policy

Definition: A topic statement that urges a person, group, or government to take a particular action. Resolutions of policy almost always have the words "should" or "ought to" in them.

Example: "RESOLVED: That the United States should change its policy in Africa" is a *resolution of policy* because it urges that a particular action be taken—a change in U.S. policy in Africa.

See also: HIGH SCHOOL POLICY DEBATE, NDT DEBATE, RESOLU-
TION, RESOLUTION OF FACT, RESOLUTION OF QUASI-
POLICY, RESOLUTION OF VALUE

resolution of quasi-policy
Definition: A topic statement that makes an evaluation of a policy.
Example: "RESOLVED: That the zero tolerance policy is not effec-
tive" is considered a *quasi-policy resolution* because it evalu-
ates the policy of zero tolerance towards drugs.
See also: RESOLUTION, RESOLUTION OF FACT, RESOLUTION OF
POLICY, RESOLUTION OF VALUE

resolution of value
Definition: A topic statement that makes a subjective evaluation of an
event, idea, person, place, or thing.
Example: "RESOLVED: That civil disobedience is good" is a *resolution of value* because it makes an evaluation of civil disobedience. It is a subjective evaluation of civil disobedience
because it requires opinions or beliefs about civil disobedience.
See also: RESOLUTION, RESOLUTION OF FACT, RESOLUTION OF
POLICY, RESOLUTION OF QUASI-POLICY

resolutional standard
Definition: A competitiveness standard that argues that if the counterplan or value alternative is the opposite of the resolution,
then it is competitive with the plan or value example.
Example: "Our counterplan to increase aid to freedom fighters is
competitive with the plan to stop aid to the Contras because
it is directly the opposite of the resolution 'RESOLVED:
That the United States should cut aid to foreign rebel
groups.' "
Note: This is not considered a strong competitiveness standard by
many theorists.
See also: COMPETITIVENESS, COUNTERPLAN, MUTUAL EXCLU-
SIVITY, NET BENEFITS, PERMUTATION

respond
Definition: To answer; to argue against.

Example: A person *responds* in cross-examination by answering questions. A person *responds* in a speech by arguing against an opponent's argument.

See also: CLASH, COUNTERARGUMENT, REFUTATION, RESPONSE

respondent

Definition: The person who answers questions during cross-examination.

Example: Questioner: "How will you enforce your plan?" *Respondent:* "We will use all constitutional means, including fines and imprisonment."

See also: CROSS-EXAMINATION, QUESTIONER, RESPOND, RESPONSE

response

Definition: An answer to a question; an argument against an opposing argument.

Usage: I have two responses to the value objection. *(I will make two arguments against their value objection.)*

See also: CLASH, COUNTERARGUMENT, REFUTATION, RESPOND

retort

Definition: To make a witty response.

Example: To the question "Do you have any solvency?" a good *retort* might be "Well, outside of the seven pieces of evidence we read, I guess not."

See also: HUMOR, RESPOND

reveal

Definition: Occurs when a judge tells which team he or she voted for prior to the end of a tournament. A judge might reveal his or her decision right after a debate round, or the judge might reveal the decision to a coach.

Usage: Do you reveal? *(Do you give your decision prior to the end of a tournament?)*

Note: Many tournaments explicitly ask judges not to reveal their decision.

See also: ORAL CRITIQUE, ORAL DECISION

reverse voting issue

Definition: To make an issue favor one's position instead of one's opponent's.

Usage: Topicality is a reverse voter. *(The affirmative is arguing that if they can show that their value example or plan supports the resolution, they should win the debate, irrespective of other issues in the debate.)*

See also: JURISDICTION, JUSTIFICATION, TOPICALITY, TURN-AROUND, VOTING ISSUE

rhetoric

Definition: The use of any ethical means to effectively convey a message to an audience, including style, argument, organization, and delivery.

See also: ARGUMENTATION, PERSUASION

risk

Definition: The dangers of accepting a belief or taking an action.

Example: Implementing a new, large program of aid to Israel may carry *risks* of angering Arabs and hurting sectors of the Israeli economy. Believing in the value of human rights may carry the *risk* of government instability and, perhaps, war.

See also: PRESUMPTION, SYSTEMS ANALYSIS

risk assessment

Definition: A process of determining the risks associated with a change in values or policy. One might do a risk assessment by looking at the seriousness of a problem, the amount of change considered, the ability to reverse that change, and the accuracy of the assessment of the situation.

See also: POLICY SYSTEMS, PRESUMPTION, SYSTEMS ANALYSIS, VALUE

risk of the resolution

Definition: The belief that the resolution may be dangerous. The risk of the resolution always gives presumption to the negative because the negative is against the resolution and therefore avoids the resolution's risks.

Example: Accepting the resolution "RESOLVED: That cars should be made non-polluting" presents certain risks—for example, harm to the economy, or improper pollution control devices—and therefore the resolution should not be supported until proven solidly by the affirmative.

See also: HYPOTHESIS TESTING, PRESUMPTION

Robert's Rules of Order

Definition: Standards and guidelines for appropriate parliamentary procedure. Included in *Robert's Rules of Order* are rules on how many votes are needed to pass a motion, what to do when an amendment is made to a main motion, and more.

See also: STUDENT CONGRESS

Rostrum

Definition: A publication of the National Forensic League that promotes high school speech and debate. It includes articles on forensics and award-winning teams and speakers.

See also: FORENSIC QUARTERLY

rules

Definition: Agreed-upon expectations of behavior for debates.

Example: While judges vary, certain *rules* are virtually unanimously agreed upon, including: There are time limits; there is an affirmative and a negative team; and the judge is the final decisionmaker.

See also: DECISION RULE

run

Definition: To argue; to support a position.

Usage: What are you running? *(What arguments or positions do you support in your debates?;* or *What case do you support in your debates?)* I'm going to run that catalytic converter value objection. *(I will argue a value objection about catalytic converters.)*

See also: ARGUE

S

sandbagging

Definition: To present a weak argument so that an opponent will respond with arguments that can easily be beaten.

Example: Team Z *sandbags* by making a weak argument that current toxic waste management programs are inadequate to deal with the toxic waste problem so that their opponent will argue that current programs work. Team Z *sandbags* because they want their opponents to waste time making "the status quo works" arguments that they can easily beat.

Usage: That was the worst case of sandbagging I've seen in a long time. *(Team X presented a really weak argument so that their opponents would respond to it. Their opponents were beaten back by strong responses by Team X.)*

See also: MULTIPLE RESPONSES, SCATTER, SKELETON, SPREAD, STRATEGY

scatter

Definition: To make many different arguments against an argument or case. A team would scatter if they made seven different responses against each affirmative-case argument.

See also: MULTIPLE RESPONSES, SANDBAGGING, SPREAD, STRATEGY

scouting

Definition: The process of finding out what other debaters' cases and arguments are. At a tournament, a person scouting might ask other debaters and judges to say the arguments or give notes on the arguments of other teams.

See also: FLOW

second affirmative constructive

Definition: The speech in team debate that follows the first negative speaker. Included in a second affirmative constructive in a debate might be the following elements: a quick introduction, answers to any negative offcase arguments, a rebuilding of the affirmative case, and then a conclusion.

See also: DIVISION OF LABOR, EMORY SWITCH, FIRST AFFIRMATIVE, FIRST AFFIRMATIVE CONSTRUCTIVE, FIRST AFFIRMATIVE REBUTTAL, SECOND AFFIRMATIVE REBUTTAL, SECOND AFFIRMATIVE SPEAKER

second affirmative rebuttal

Definition: The last speech of a team debate in which the affirmative attempts to answer the second negative rebuttal's arguments and to give the judge reasons to vote for the affirmative. Included in a second affirmative rebuttal might be the following: an introduction, explanations of why the affirmative is winning each of the offcase or planside and caseside issues, a summary of why the affirmative is winning overall, and then a conclusion.

See also: DIVISION OF LABOR, INSIDE-OUTSIDE, SECOND AFFIRMATIVE CONSTRUCTIVE, SECOND AFFIRMATIVE SPEAKER

second affirmative speaker

Definition: The speaker in team debate who gives the second affirmative constructive and, usually, the second affirmative rebuttal.

Synonym: SECOND AFFIRMATIVE

See also: DIVISION OF LABOR, INSIDE-OUTSIDE, SECOND AFFIRMATIVE CONSTRUCTIVE, SECOND AFFIRMATIVE REBUTTAL, SPEAKER DUTIES

second level arguments

Definition: Arguments that take into consideration opposing arguments. Second level arguments are frequently used in rebuttal speeches because the rebuttal speaker must consider the opponent's arguments.

Example: Instead of arguing that a plan will stop proliferation, a team makes a *second level argument:* "The plan will slow proliferation, and, if proliferation does occur, will make it safe." This is a *second level argument* because it considers the argument that proliferation may be good.

See also: MULTIPLE LEVEL ARGUMENTS

second negative constructive

Definition: The speech in a team debate following the second affirmative speaker in which, traditionally, the negative makes arguments against the plan (policy debate) or the value example supported by the affirmative (value debate). Included in a typical high school policy second negative constructive might be the following: an introduction; solvency, workability, and disadvantage arguments; and a conclusion. In a typical NDT policy debate, a second negative constructive might include the following: a quick introduction; a rebuilding of offcase arguments (like counterplans, topicality, and disadvantages) originally made in the first negative constructive; new arguments, such as more disadvantages; and a conclusion. In CEDA debate, the typical second negative constructive includes the following: introduction; a rebuilding of the negative counter criteria and attacks on the affirmative criteria; an argument of two or three value objections or countervalue arguments; and a conclusion.

See also: DIVISION OF LABOR, EMORY SWITCH, SECOND NEGATIVE SPEAKER, SECOND NEGATIVE REBUTTAL, SPEAKER DUTIES

second negative rebuttal

Definition: The speech in team debate that follows the first affirmative rebuttal. A typical second negative rebuttal might include: an introduction, a rebuilding of offcase arguments (topicality arguments, disadvantages, and counterplans in policy debate; value objections and countervalues in value debate), a restatement of why the affirmative case arguments are not valid, and then a summary of why the negative should win the debate.

See also: DIVISION OF LABOR, REBUTTAL, SECOND NEGATIVE CONSTRUCTIVE, SECOND NEGATIVE SPEAKER, SPEAKER DUTIES

second negative speaker

Definition: The speaker who gives the second negative constructive and second negative rebuttal speeches.

Synonym: SECOND NEGATIVE

See also: DIVISION OF LABOR, EMORY SWITCH, SECOND NEGATIVE CONSTRUCTIVE, SECOND NEGATIVE REBUTTAL, SPEAKER DUTIES

secondary source

Definition: A source of a quotation who is not directly involved in the issue that the quotation addresses.

Example: When William F. Buckley comments on civil rights cases before the Supreme Court, he is a *secondary source* because he is not directly involved in the cases.

See also: EVIDENCE, EXPERT, PRIMARY SOURCE, SOURCE

section

See: PLANK

senior division

Definition: A group of debate teams with two or more years of experience that compete against each other at a debate tournament.

See also: DIVISION, TOURNAMENT

sever

Definition: To no longer support a part of one's case or plan.

Example: An affirmative team argued that we should switch from fossil fuels to solar and nuclear power. The negative made very strong arguments against nuclear power. So, the affirmative *severed* nuclear power from its plan in the first affirmative rebuttal and supported solar power only from that point on in the debate.

Usage: We will sever plank two, portions A, C, and D. *(We will no longer support the parts of the plan contained in parts A, C, and D, presumably because they will cause disadvantages.)*

See also: AMEND, DISCO, HYPOTHESIS TESTING

shift

Definition: To change one's position or argument in later speeches. Shifting is usually considered an illegitimate practice, especially in the last rebuttal speeches.

Example: In the first affirmative constructive, a team originally argues that poverty is a growing problem and then, in the first affirmative rebuttal, the team *shifts* the argument to "A lack of jobs is a growing problem."

Usage: She totally shifted in her rebuttal. *(She changed the arguments that her team had originally presented in their first speech.)*

See also: SEVER

shift of opinion debate

Definition: A debate that is judged by people who state their opinion on the topic before the debate and then state their opinion on the topic after the debate. The team that shifts more opinions to their side wins the debate.

See also: BALLOT, DEBATE FORMATS, JUDGE

shotgun

Definition: A very rapid style of delivery. A debater who shotguns presents many arguments and goes very fast.

Usage: They shotgun when they're negative. *(They speak very rapidly and present many arguments when they debate as the negative team.)*

See also: SCATTER, SPEED, SPREAD

should

Definition: Ought to, but not necessarily will. "Should" is often used in policy resolutions.

Example: Under the resolution "RESOLVED: That the United States *should* curtail arms sales to foreign countries significantly," the affirmative would need to show that the United

States ought to curtail arms, even though the United States might not actually do so.

See also: RESOLUTION OF POLICY, SHOULD-COULD FALLACY, SHOULD-WOULD FALLACY

should-could fallacy

Definition: A flawed argument that states that because the present system can resolve a problem or can achieve an advantage or can enact the affirmative plan, we should not enact a plan that would solve the problem.

Example: A *should-could fallacy* would be this argument: "Because Congress could pass the affirmative plan, the status quo can solve the problem, so we don't need the affirmative plan." Another *should-could fallacy* would be "There are many programs that could solve the illiteracy problem; therefore, we should not enact the affirmative plan."

See also: INHERENCY, PLANSIDE BARRIER, SHOULD-WOULD FALLACY

should-would fallacy

Definition: A flawed argument that shows that the affirmative plan will not be passed into action, and that we, therefore, should not enact the affirmative plan.

Example: "Congress is against the affirmative plan, so it will never pass into law." "The affirmative plan is unconstitutional, so it will never be permitted." Both of these negative arguments are *should-would fallacies* because they state that the plan would not be passed, not should not be passed.

See also: FIAT, SHOULD-COULD FALLACY

sign reasoning

Definition: To conclude that an event or fact is true because specific facts have been established or because specific events have occurred.

Example: "Because there are so many books in this building and because they are ordered according to the Library of Congress numbers, this must, therefore, be a library."

See also: LOGIC, REASONING

significance

Definition: The issue of whether there is an important problem and harms in the present system; the need for a plan or advantage.

Example: A mini-debate on *significance.*

Affirmative: "Cigarette smoking is pervasive, and it is causing thousands of deaths each year."

Negative: "Cigarette smoking is decreasing, and it does not cause all that many deaths."

Usage: They have no significance. *(They have not shown there is a significant problem.)*

Synonym: NEED

See also: HARMS, STOCK ISSUES

skeleton

Definition: A minimally supported main argument.

Example: A *skeleton* disadvantage has just two or three pieces of evidence and as many subpoints:

I. Increasing agricultural subsidies will hurt the economy.
   A. The economy is unstable.
   B. Increased subsidies will hurt foreign markets for U.S. goods.
   C. Hurting foreign markets will bring us into economic recession.

See also: SANDBAGGING

skills judge

Definition: A judge who makes decisions based on the quality of the debaters' arguments and speaking skills. During the debate, a skills judge will carefully watch the speakers to see how well they debate. A skills judge's decision is not based on the content of the arguments presented, but rather on how well the arguments are presented.

See also: DELIVERY, JUDGE, PARADIGM

slug

See: LABEL

solvency

Definition: The issue of whether a plan or value object will solve a problem, achieve an advantage, or meet a goal or criterion.

Example: A mini-debate on *solvency*.

Affirmative: Our worksharing plan will gain the advantage of giving millions of people new jobs.

Negative: Worksharing will lead to an economic downturn and thereby actually decrease employment.

See also: ADVANTAGE, STOCK ISSUES, WORKABILITY

solvency-disadvantage contradiction

See: SOLVENCY-DISADVANTAGE DILEMMA

solvency-disadvantage dilemma

Definition: Occurs when a solvency argument contradicts a disadvantage.

Example: A team would be in a *solvency-disadvantage dilemma* if they first argued that national health insurance will fail to solve the lack of medical care because people won't go to the doctor anyway, and then argued a disadvantage that too many people will actually go to the doctor, creating hospital overloads.

Synonym: SOLVENCY-DISADVANTAGE CONTRADICTION

See also: CONTRADICTION, DILEMMA, INHERENCY-DISADVANTAGE DILEMMA

solvency-inherency contradiction

See: SOLVENCY-INHERENCY DILEMMA

solvency-inherency dilemma

Definition: Occurs when a solvency argument contradicts an inherency argument.

Example: A team would be in a *solvency-inherency dilemma* if they first argued that current programs to give money to the poor work and then argued that the affirmative plan, which gives money to the poor, won't work.

Synonym: SOLVENCY-INHERENCY CONTRADICTION

See also: INHERENCY-DISADVANTAGE DILEMMA, SOLVENCY-DISADVANTAGE DILEMMA

sophistry

Definition: The use of persuasion based on appeals to an audience.

See also: APPEAL, DIALECTIC, PATHOS

sound argument

Definition: An argument that is well supported.

Example: A *sound argument* might be "Crack is dangerous because studies show that it creates addiction and can kill."

See also: EVIDENCE, TOULMIN MODEL OF ARGUMENT

source

Definition: An author; the authors; their qualifications; name of periodical, book, document, or newspaper; date of publication; and page number of an evidence quote.

Example: Clay Shaw, U.S. Representative from Florida, *Congressional Record,* June 26, 1986, pg. E2320.

Usage: Who's your source? *(Who are the authors of that evidence and what are their qualifications?)*

See also: EVIDENCE, HEARSAY, PRIMARY SOURCE

speaker

Definition: A person who orally communicates to an audience. Debaters are speakers because they speak to their judges— they orally present their arguments.

See also: COMMUNICATION, DEBATE, DELIVERY

Speaker and Gavel

Definition: A journal that features articles on debate and speech published by the college speech organization Delta Sigma Rho–Tau Kappa Alpha.

See also: ARGUMENTATION AND ADVOCACY, CEDA YEARBOOK, FORENSIC

speaker awards

Definition: Recognition or trophies for the top debaters at tournaments. At some tournaments, the top three, five, or ten debaters, based on speaker points and rankings, are given speaker awards.

See also: RANK, RATING, SPEAKER POINTS

speaker duties

Definition: The issues that a debater should argue in his or her speech. There are various duties for speakers, but essentially each speaker responds to the previous opponent's arguments, with the following exceptions: 1) when the first affirmative constructive presents the affirmative case; 2) when the second or first negative speakers present offcase arguments; 3) when in team debate, the first negative rebuttal argues the issues that the second negative constructive did not argue. The first affirmative rebuttal responds to both the first negative rebuttal and second negative constructive.

Usage: The negative needs to learn the speaker duties. *(The negative needs to divide their duties so that they do not argue the same thing. The first negative rebuttal should argue different issues than the second negative constructive.)*

See also: DIVISION OF LABOR, FIRST AFFIRMATIVE CONSTRUCTIVE, FIRST AFFIRMATIVE REBUTTAL, FIRST NEGATIVE CONSTRUCTIVE, FIRST NEGATIVE REBUTTAL, SECOND AFFIRMATIVE CONSTRUCTIVE, SECOND AFFIRMATIVE REBUTTAL, SECOND NEGATIVE CONSTRUCTIVE, SECOND NEGATIVE REBUTTAL, SPEAKER ORDER

speaker order

Definition: The order in which debaters speak.
Example: In team debate the order is:

1AC: 8 or 10 minutes	2NC: 8 or 10 minutes
1AC is questioned by 2NC	2NC is questioned by 2AC
1NC: 8 or 10 minutes	1NR: 4 or 5 minutes
1NC is questioned by 1AC	1AR: 4 or 5 minutes
2AC: 8 or 10 minutes	2NR: 4 or 5 minutes
2AC is questioned by 1NC	2AR: 4 or 5 minutes

In Lincoln-Douglas debate the order is:

1AC: 6 or 7 minutes	1AR: 4 minutes
1AC is questioned by Neg.	1NR: 6 minutes
1NC: 7 or 8 minutes	2AR: 3 minutes

1NC is questioned by Aff.
Question periods last three minutes.

See also: EMORY SWITCH, INSIDE-OUTSIDE, SPEAKER DUTIES

speaker points

Definition: The total number of points a debater receives from judge ratings in a debate round or during preliminary rounds at a tournament.

Example: With thirty possible *speaker points* given by a judge each round, a debater could have a maximum of 180 *speaker points* after six rounds of debate.

Usage: How many points did you have at that tournament? *(How many points from judge ratings did you have during preliminary rounds at that tournament?)* What kind of speaks did that judge give you? *(How many speaker points did that judge give you?)*

Synonyms: POINTS, SPEAKS
See also: SPEAKER AWARDS

speaks
See: SPEAKER POINTS

specialization
See: CLASSIFICATION

spike

Definition: An addition to the plan that allows the plan to gain its advantage or to prevent a disadvantage.

Example: If a plan were to significantly reduce military spending, the plan could include a *spike* providing a jobs program, in order to prevent the plan from causing large amounts of unemployment.

See also: DISADVANTAGE, PLAN

spread

Definition: To present many arguments, usually at a rapid rate.

Usage: He tries to spread but he just mushmouths. *(He tries to speak quickly and present many arguments, but he slurs his words and is hard to understand.)*

See also: COMMUNICATION, DELIVERY, SCATTER, SHOTGUN

squad

Definition: A school's debaters and speakers

Example: The John F. Kennedy High School *squad* had four debate teams and sixteen individual events speakers.

Synonym: TEAM (2)

See also: TEAM (1)

squirrel case

Definition: An unusual affirmative case.

Example: A *squirrel case* on the resolution "RESOLVED: That the United States should implement a comprehensive agricultural policy" was to stop killer bees. It was considered a *squirrel case* because it was unusual—it wasn't a case that people would automatically think of in support of that resolution.

See also: PERIPHERAL ARGUMENT, TOPICALITY

stalemate

Definition: An unbreakable tie on an argument or issue.

Example: One team may have evidence showing crime is going up, while another team may have evidence showing crime is going down. A *stalemate* would occur if neither side could show which evidence was superior.

stance

See: STAND ON AN ISSUE

stand on an issue

Definition: To support a position on an important area of argument.

Example: To oppose the right to abortion, to oppose the right to abortion in certain instances like rape and incest, or to support the right to abortion are all possible *stands* on the abortion issue.

Usage: What's your stand (or stance) on the economic growth issue? *(What position do you agree with on the economic growth issue?)*

See also: PHILOSOPHY, POSITION

standard

Definition: A rule that ought to be met.

Example: A legal *standard* for topicality argues that legal sources provide the best definitions.

Usage: What standard are you using to show that cars are dangerous enough to be banned? *(What rule, what level of proof of the danger of cars, do you believe is needed to show that cars should be banned?)*

See also: DECISION RULE, TOPICALITY

stasis

Definition: The key areas of disagreement.

Example: If a team supported a national college student loan and grant program and their opponents were against such a program, then the *stasis* could center on whether such loans would help students, be too costly, or increase minority involvement in schools.

See also: COMPETITIVENESS, ISSUES, UNIQUENESS

status quo

Definition: The present system; the current situation; current government, private industry, and group policies.

Example: Today, many people use cars and drive on superfreeways. This is the *status quo.* The U.S. use of executive, legislative, and judicial branches is the *status quo* as well, since this is our present system of government. In policy debate, affirmative teams support policies to change the *status quo;* for example, to change the executive branch.

Usage: Can the status quo solve the toxic waste problem? *(Can the current government and private industry policies deal with the toxic waste problem?)*

See also: DEFENSE OF THE STATUS QUO, INHERENCY

stock issues

Definition: The traditional issues of a debate.

Example: In policy debate the *stock issues* are 1) topicality (does the plan follow and justify the resolution?); 2) significance (is there a significant problem?); 3) inherency (is the present system unable to resolve the problem?); 4) solvency (will the plan solve the problem?); 5) disadvantages (will the plan create new problems that outweigh the present system's problems?). In value debate, the *stock issues* are 1) definitive (what proof must be shown to justify the resolution?); 2) designative (is there sufficient proof to justify the resolution?); 3) justification (does the affirmative case support the resolution?).

See also: HYPOTHESIS TESTING, PARADIGM, STOCK ISSUES PARADIGM, SYSTEMS ANALYSIS

stock issues paradigm

Definition: A view of debate that requires the affirmative to win each stock issue. In a policy debate, with a judge who uses the stock issues paradigm, the affirmative must show 1) that there is a significant problem; 2) that the present system will not solve the problem; 3) that the affirmative plan will solve this problem; 4) that the plan will not cause new problems that are worse than the plan's advantages; and 5) that their plan supports the topic. In a value debate, with a judge who uses the stock issues paradigm, the affirmative must properly evaluate the terms in the resolution and how to prove those terms. The affirmative also must see that the value object proves those terms, and that their case supports the resolution. If the affirmative loses one stock issue, using the stock issue paradigm, the negative wins the debate.

See also: PARADIGM

straight refutation

Definition: A negative strategy that refutes and makes some counterarguments against an affirmative case but never takes a counterposition.

Example: Against an affirmative case that supported a decrease in military spending, the negative, using *straight refutation,* would argue that the affirmative hadn't proven their case and that there was no need to cut military spending; but they would not support any particular amount of military spending.

See also: HYPOTHESIS TESTING

strategy

Definition: An approach to arguing or speaking, or any planned use of technique that debaters follow to win.

Usage: What's your strategy for your next debate? *(What arguments will you support in order to win the debate?)*

strawperson fallacy

Definition: To misrepresent an opponent's argument so that the argument appears weak and is easy to respond to.

Example: After the negative carefully supported privacy from random strip searches, the affirmative made this *strawperson fallacy:* "Now the negative is saying that all privacy is important; so, they are supporting the right of drug dealers to deal in privacy."

See also: FALLACY, SANDBAGGING

structural barrier

Definition: An inherency argument that the laws of the present system are legally different from the affirmative plan.

Example: An affirmative may argue that there are laws that allow the death penalty in forty states. These laws are *structural barriers* to an affirmative plan that would ban the death penalty.

Note: A structural barrier is *not* a law stopping the affirmative plan from being enacted (see SHOULD-COULD FALLACY, SHOULD-WOULD FALLACY).

See also: INHERENCY, INHERENT BARRIER, PLANSIDE BARRIER, STRUCTURAL INHERENCY

structural inherency

Definition: An argument that the laws of the present system prevent a solution to a problem or the achievement of an advantage.

Example: An affirmative *structural inherency* argument might be that current laws allowing some trade with South Africa will not resolve the apartheid problem in South Africa.

Synonym: STRUCTURE (2)

See also: INHERENCY, STRUCTURAL BARRIER

structure (1)
See: ORGANIZATION

structure (2)
See: STRUCTURAL INHERENCY

student congress
Definition: A forensic event that allows students to engage in parliamentary debate by imitating a congressional session.
See also: ROBERT'S RULES OF ORDER

student judge
Definition: A judge who is a student in the same grade level as the debaters he or she is judging. At some tournaments, experienced debaters act as student judges by judging beginning debaters.
See also: JUDGE

study counterplan
Definition: A negative plan to study the problem or affirmative plan.
Example: A *study counterplan* against an acid rain case concludes that instead of using scrubbers on coal plants to reduce acid rain, acid rain and scrubbers should both be studied.
See also: COUNTERPLAN, PROCESS COUNTERPLAN

style
Definition: The use of appealing language that makes a speech or case more persuasive; the unique qualities of a debater's delivery, arguments, and language. The use of metaphors or twists of phrase would qualify as style. A debater's sense of humor and blunt, to-the-point arguments might be considered that debater's style.
See also: DELIVERY, LANGUAGE

sub-issue
Definition: An issue that supports a larger, main issue.
Example: *Sub-issues* of the death penalty issue include whether it is cruel and unusual punishment, whether it prevents further crime, whether it is racially biased, and whether it actually saves money.
See also: ISSUE, SUBORDINATION

subordination

Definition: To make sub-arguments that support main arguments; a more important and more general argument that is supported by more specific and smaller arguments.

Example: If one were to argue that garage doors hurt children because garage doors cost money and because garage doors are not a good idea, one would be incorrectly *subordinating*. The main argument, "Garage doors hurt children," is not supported by "Garage doors cost money." To properly *subordinate* the argument, one would need to argue that garage doors are not a good idea because they hurt children and are expensive.

See also: DEDUCTION, OUTLINE ORGANIZATION

substantive

Definition: To be a well supported and relevant argument, issue, or debate. A substantive debate would be one where relevant issues were debated and where arguments were well supported.

See also: EVIDENCE

sub-topicality

See: JUSTIFICATION (3)

summarize

Definition: To review previous points and arguments.

Example: "In *summary*, there are three issues in this debate: the advantage of more jobs, and the two disadvantages of higher crime and increased inflation."

See also: SYNTHESIS

support

Definition: The reasoned proof for an argument or position.

Example: By using evidence one can *support* an argument. To quote Ted Kennedy when he said that census reports document that there are 3.5 million elderly in poverty would *support* the argument that over three million elderly live in poverty. When debaters state the reason for an argument, they *support* that argument; for example, "Television hurts study habits because students watch television instead of studying."

See also: BACKING, DOCUMENTATION, EVIDENCE, WARRANT

sweeps
See: SWEEPSTAKES AWARD

sweepstakes award
Definition: A trophy or some other form of recognition for the school squad that did the best at a tournament according to that tournament's rules.

Example: A tournament might give from one to forty points for debate teams and individual events speakers that do exceptionally well. The school squad that garners the most points wins the *sweepstakes award.*

Usage: Who won sweeps? *(Which school squad won the trophy for being best at the tournament?)*

See also: SQUAD, TEAM

syllogism
Definition: An argument that follows the form "Given $a = b$ and $b = c$, then $a = c$."

Example: Given that schools that educate ineffectively should be reformed, and given that school C does educate ineffectively, then school C should be reformed.

See also: CONCLUSION, ENTHYMEME, MAJOR PREMISE, MINOR PREMISE

symposium style debate
See: PORTLAND STYLE DEBATE

synthesis
Definition: To show why the issues and arguments of a debate lead to one conclusion.

Example: "Since we have shown that jobs are most important because people need to work for self-worth and even for their health, and because the affirmative does not increase crime and barely increases inflation, you should vote for the affirmative jobs program."

See also: SUMMARIZE

systems analysis

Definition: A view that debates are comparisons between the affirmative and negative positions. In policy debate, decisions are based upon three main issues: topicality, advantages, and disadvantages. If the topical plan advantages outweigh the disadvantages, then the affirmative wins. In value debate, decisions also are based upon three main issues: topicality, value supports, and value objections. If the topical value example supports outweigh the objections, then the affirmative wins.

See also: HYPOTHESIS TESTING, POLICY SYSTEMS, STOCK ISSUES, VALUE

"T"

See: TOPICALITY

tab room

See: TABULATION ROOM

tabula rasa

Definition: A view of debate that promotes judging without any bias toward any argument that debaters present. Tabula rasa judges attempt to listen without bias to any argument, including ones like "Nuclear war is good" and "Economic growth is bad," even if they do not agree with such arguments.

See also: CRITIC OF ARGUMENT, GAMESPLAYER, INTERVENTION, PARADIGM

tabulation room

Definition: The place where tournament directors collect ballots, record decisions and speaker points, and then match teams to debate each other.

Usage: Who's in the tab room? *(Who are the tournament directors recording and matching debates?)*

See also: MATCHING, TOURNAMENT

take out

Definition: To completely defeat an opposing argument.

Example: Team X took out team Y's high cost argument by showing the plan actually saved money.

Synonym: KICKS OUT

See also: KICKED OUT, KICKS IN

team (1)

Definition: One to four persons who debate together. In Lincoln-Douglas debate, one person debates as a team. In other forms of debate, two, three, or four persons debate as a team, although only two debate at a time.

Usage: Who is your top team? *(Which persons debating together are your best?)*

See also: LINCOLN-DOUGLAS DEBATE

team (2)

See: SQUAD

team debate

Definition: A debate where each side has two or more members. In high school policy, CEDA, and NDT debate, each side has two members, so these types of debates are team debates.

See also: ONE-PERSON DEBATE, TEAM (1)

teamwork

Definition: To work together effectively. On many squads, debaters work together to help each other practice speaking, research, make cases, and become better debaters and speakers.

See also: SQUAD

technicality

Definition: A small argument; a procedural issue.

Example: Despite two large and well developed disadvantages, a judge votes for the affirmative because they won a reverse voting issue on topicality. Some might feel that this is a *technicality.*

See also: DECISION, PARADIGM, REASON FOR DECISION

terminal value
Definition: A type of value that is an end.
Example: The instrumental value of using preventive medicine might lead to a *terminal value:* saving lives.
See also: INSTRUMENTAL VALUE, VALUE

terms
Definition: Words in the resolution.
Example: The *terms* in a resolution might be "Resolved," "That," "taxes," "should," "be," and "increased."
Usage: The affirmative is not following the terms of the topic. *(The affirmative is not dealing with the resolution as they should; the affirmative is not topical.)* We will define the terms in the resolution. *(We will define the words in the topic of debate.)*
See also: RESOLUTION, TOPICALITY

testimony
Definition: Evidence that comes from someone who spoke in a hearing or courtroom.
Example: When people presented reports or answered questions during the Robert Bork hearings, their presentations were *testimony.*
See also: EVIDENCE, PRIMARY SOURCE

theme
Definition: The main idea behind a series of arguments or positions.
Example: An affirmative might argue that economic growth leads to better jobs, more jobs, higher wages, and safer working conditions. A *theme* behind these arguments is that economic growth helps working people.
See also: PHILOSOPHY, POSITION, THESIS

theory
Definition: Disputable ideas about the practice or assumptions of debate. There are many theories about debate. For example, there are at least four major theories concerning presumption. There are also theories about topicality, competitive counterplans, and debate's purpose.
See also: PARADIGM

thesis

Definition: The main point of a speech; what will be proven in a speech; the main idea of an argument.

Example: "In my speech, I will show that boxing should be banned."

Usage: What's the thesis of your argument? *(What is the main point of your argument?)*

Synonym: (for the third definition) THEME

See also: RESOLUTION

three-person team

Definition: Three people who debate together. Two of the three people debate on the affirmative, and one of those two and the third person debate on the negative.

See also: FOUR-PERSON TEAM, TEAM

threshold

See: BRINK

time (1)

Definition: The amount of minutes and seconds in a speech. There are time limits for speeches in a debate. A timekeeper keeps the time in a debate.

Usage: How much time is left? *(How many minutes and seconds remain in the speech?)*

See also: PREPARATION TIME, SPEAKER ORDER, TIME (2)

time (2)

Definition: An indication that the speaker has no speaking or preparation time remaining.

Usage: Time. *(The end of a speech; no more time left)*

See also: PREPARATION TIME, TIME (1), TIME SIGNAL, TIME-KEEPER

time signal

Definition: A hand gesture or written or oral statement of how much time remains in a speech. Time signals usually include five fingers for five minutes remaining in the speech, four fingers for four minutes remaining, and so on, until half a minute is indicated by a bent finger; a fist or "T" created by both hands intersecting shows there is no time left.

See also: TIME (2), TIMEKEEPER

timekeeper

Definition: The person who keeps track of time, telling speakers how much time remains in their speeches and how much preparation time remains.

Example: A *timekeeper* gives time signals during speeches and cross-examination periods, and when debaters are using preparation time, orally tells the debaters how much preparation time a team has remaining.

See also: TIME (1), TIME (2), TIME SIGNAL

topic

See: RESOLUTION

topicality

Definition: In policy debate, the issue of whether the affirmative plan supports the resolution; in value debate, the issue of whether the value example supports the resolution.

Example: A plan to ban car sales to Chile does not support the resolution "RESOLVED: That car sales to Iran should be banned" because it does not ban sales to Iran as the topic says. The plan is therefore not topical. If in a value debate the resolution was "RESOLVED: That elite power is the most important value" and the affirmative argued that democracy is the most important value, they would not support the resolution because supporting democracy (a value example) does not support elite power, and, therefore, the case is not topical.

Synonyms: RESOLUTIONALITY, "T"

See also: JUSTIFICATION, PLAN, TYPICALITY, VALUE EXAMPLE

topicality by effect

See: EFFECTS-TOPICALITY

Toulmin model of argument

Definition: A diagram of the essential elements of an argument, including the claim, data, warrant, backing, reservation, and qualifier. The claim is the conclusion, the main point of the argument. The data is the evidence for the argument. The warrant states that the evidence supports the argument. The reservation is the limitation, or the exceptions to the claim. The qualifier is the strength of the claim. The backing is the support for the warrant.

Example: Given the *data:* Solar power is environmentally safe

We can *claim:* The government should encourage solar power

Unless *reservation:* Doing so would be too costly

Since *warrant:* We should encourage environmentally safe energy

Qualifier: To a certain degree

Because *backing:* Fossil fuels are damaging the ozone, yet people still need energy to get to work and to have heat in their homes.

See also: BACKING, CLAIM, DATA, QUALIFIER, RESERVATION, WARRANT

tournament

Definition: A series of debates or individual speaking events between teams from different schools. Tournments usually have between ten and fifty schools, with many competing teams and speakers.

Synonym: TOURNEY

See also: DIVISION, MATCHING, TABLUATION ROOM

tourney

See: TOURNAMENT

transition

Definition: A connection between ideas in a speech or arguments in a case.

Example: "In addition to the injuries, we also note the thousands of deaths in subpoint B . . . ."

See also: CASE, STYLE

trend

Definition: A movement toward some end.

Example: There is a *trend* toward "back to basics" in American schools because more and more American schools are teaching fundamental skills.

Usage: The trend in the status quo to use competitive bidding will solve the military procurement misuse. *(The increasing use of and movement toward competitive bidding will prevent military procurement misuse.)*

See also: INCREMENTALISM

turkey

Definition: To vote in the minority in a debate.

Example: If two of three judges in a debate vote for one team, and the other judge, judge X, votes for the other team, then judge X *turkeyed.*

Usage: Who turkeyed in that round? *(Who was the judge in the minority in the decision for that debate?)*

See also: JUDGE, OUTROUNDS

turn

See: TURNAROUND

turnaround

Definition: A response that makes an opponent's argument support your position.

Example: A *turnaround* to the argument that a plan will hurt the economy is "The plan will actually help our economy."

Usage: I ran a turnaround against their disadvantage. *(I argued that their disadvantage actually supported our arguments. It supported our case.)* They had a good turnaround against our value objection. *(The affirmative had a good argument showing that the affirmative value actually had good effects and was therefore not objectionable.)*

Synonyms: FLIP, TURN

See also: CLASH, REFUTATION, TURNING THE TABLES

turning the tables

Definition: To use your opponent's arguments or evidence to support your own position.

Example: You support state action and your opponents support federal action to improve water quality. However, you notice that in your opponent's case there is a piece of evidence that says states are needed to resolve the water problem. You could *turn the tables* on your opponents and use their own evidence to support your case.

See also: CLASH, REFUTATION, TURNAROUND

two-speaker debate

See: ONE-PERSON DEBATE

typicality

Definition: The issue of whether the affirmative plan (policy debate) or value example (value debate) is a representative example of the resolution.

Example: The resolution is "RESOLVED: That the United States should promote affirmative action programs." Is an affirmative plan that supports affirmative action only for Eskimos representative of promoting affirmative action programs? A debate on the *typicality* of the plan would discuss this issue.

See also: COUNTERWARRANT, HASTY GENERALIZATION, JUSTIFICATION (3), REPRESENTATIVE, TOPICALITY

U

uncertainty
Definition: Without certainty.
See: CERTAINTY

underdog
Definition: The team or debater that is expected to lose a debate.
Example: Team X has won just one round in the past three tournaments and is debating Team Y which has won eighteen rounds in a row. Team X would be considered the *underdog*.
See also: LOSS, TEAM, WIN

underview
Definition: An observation or argument that is made after a series of arguments.
Example: After developing a full advantage for using water drip irrigation, a team might present an *underview* showing that drip irrigation needs to be done now. Here is an example of a case outline with an *underview*.

Advantage: The Pepper Bill will give needed home health care.
   A. Many elderly need but cannot afford home health care.
   B. Private insurance and the government don't help.
   C. The Pepper Bill pays for and assures quality home health care.

Underview: The Pepper Bill is cost effective.

    A. Its 1.5 percent tax will pay for costs.

    B. Giving home health care prevents higher-cost nursing home care.

See also: CONTENTION, OBSERVATION, OVERVIEW

unethical

Definition: Not ethical.

See: ETHICAL

unique

See: UNIQUENESS

uniqueness

Definition: The issue of whether a plan, the present system, or a value object, respectively, is the only way something good or bad will occur. Will the plan cause an advantage or a disadvantage that the present system will not gain? Does the present system cause problems or advantages that the plan would not? Are there value supports or value objections that will occur solely because of the value object?

Example: A mini-debate on the issue of *uniqueness:*

Negative: The affirmative idea of jailing more criminals will cause a great increase in riots. This rioting would only happen if we jail more criminals.

Affirmative: Wrong! Riots will occur whether we jail more criminals or not.

Usage: That case is not unique. *(The arguments of an affirmative team are not relevant because the problems the affirmative cites will occur with or without the change they suggest.)* We beat the disadvantage on uniqueness. *(The affirmative team responded to an argument against change by stating that the disadvantage would occur with or without the change.)* We showed the value objection was unique. *(The negative's argument showed the affirmative value had unique costs that would not occur without the affirmative value.)*

See also: COUNTERVALUE, DISADVANTAGE, PLAN, PRESENT SYSTEM, STATUS QUO, VALUE EXAMPLE, VALUE OBJECT, VALUE OBJECTION

universal audience
Definition: Critics who represent an audience of rational people.
See also: PARTICULAR AUDIENCE

utilitarianism
Definition: A philosophy based on the idea that one should strive for the greatest good for the greatest number.
Example: If a plan will cause 1,200 deaths but at the same time save 1,201 lives, all other things being equal, it would be *utilitarian* to support such a plan.
See also: POLICYMAKER, SYSTEMS ANALYSIS

utility case
See: NO-NEEDS CASE

V

VA

See: VISUAL AID

VO

See: VALUE OBJECTION

vague

Definition: Unclear.

Example: The argument "This is good" is *vague* because it is not clear what "this" is, nor what "good" is.

See also: CLARIFY, VOID FOR VAGUENESS

validity

Definition: The soundness of the connection between evidence and claim.

Example: The argument, "Social Security will run out of money by the latter half of the twenty-first century because the evidence indicates that baby boomers will retire and use up all the surplus funds" is *valid*, because baby boomers' use of the funds is strongly connected with Social Security running out of money.

See also: EVIDENCE, PROBABILITY, SYLLOGISM, WARRANT

value

Definition: An ideal toward which people strive.

Example: "Saving lives is good," "support for democracy," "support for social justice," and "avoiding war is good" are four different *values*. They are *values* because they express ideals toward which people choose to strive.

Usage: What value do you support in this debate? *(What ideal do you support in this debate?)*

See also: CRITERIA, GOAL, TERMINAL VALUE, VALUE HIERARCHY

value alternative

Definition: A different value that could be supported instead of the value object or value example. Value alternatives should be non-topical and competitive with the affirmative value example.

Example: On a topic "RESOLVED: That drug testing is bad," an affirmative could show that drug testing is bad by arguing for a *value alternative*. They could argue that workers should be checked by supervisors (a *value alternative*) instead of giving workers drug tests.

Usage: We run a private insurance value alternative. *(We argue that private insurance should be used instead.)*

See also: COMPETITIVENESS, COUNTERPLAN, TOPICALITY, VALUE EXAMPLE, VALUE OBJECT

value benefits

See: VALUE SUPPORT

value example

Definition: The specific example of the value object that the affirmative supports.

Example: F-16 fighter plane sales would be a *value example* of military support for the topic "RESOLVED: That military support to nondemocratic governments is justified."

See also: PLAN, VALUE ALTERNATIVE, VALUE OBJECT

value hicrarchy

Definition: The preferential ordering of values.

Example: A *value hierarchy* might consider the value of saving lives more important than preserving democracy. The preference would be for saving lives over preserving democracy.

See also: CRITERIA, GOAL, TERMINAL VALUE, VALUE

value object

Definition: The subject of a resolution of value, fact, or quasi-policy.

Example: In the resolution "RESOLVED: That courts overemphasize criminal defendant rights," the *value object* is "courts" because that is the subject of the resolution. In the resolution "RESOLVED: That the value of social justice is overly beneficial to the poor," the *value object* is "the value of social justice."

See also: AGENT, COUNTERVALUE, RESOLUTION OF FACT, RESOLUTION OF QUASI-POLICY, RESOLUTION OF VALUE, VALUE EXAMPLE, VALUE OBJECTION

value objection

Definition: An argument that the value object or value example rejects the resolution.

Example: A *value objection* to the resolution "RESOLVED: That U.S. foreign policy supports human rights" is that U.S. foreign policy (the value object) does not support human rights. A *value objection* to the resolution "RESOLVED: That the value of liberty is a bad value" is that the value of liberty (the value object) is a good value. An example of an outline of a *value objection:*

I. U.S. foreign policy does support human rights.
   A. The danger of communism is a great threat to human rights.
   B. U.S. foreign policy helps prevent communism.
   C. Preventing communism helps support human rights.

Note: There is disagreement over the use of this term. Some feel it is better defined by this dictionary's definition of "countervalue."

See also: COUNTERVALUE, DISADVANTAGE, VALUE EXAMPLE, VALUE OBJECT, VALUE SUPPORT

value support

Definition: An argument that the value object or value example supports the resolution.

Example: A value support for the resolution "RESOLVED: That U.S. foreign policy supports human rights" is that U.S. foreign policy does support human rights by quiet diplomacy. A value support for the resolution "RESOLVED: That the value of liberty is a bad value" is that the value of liberty is a bad value because it gives the rich too many rights.

Synonym: VALUE BENEFITS

See also: ADVANTAGE, VALUE EXAMPLE, VALUE OBJECT, VALUE OBJECTION

victory

Definition: To win.

See: WIN

visual aide

Definition: An object or drawing that can be shown during a speech to illustrate a point. Posters, large photos, and charts are all used as visual aids in speeches. Sometimes speakers will show the object they are talking about; for example, one speaker uses a Rubik's Cube in his speech. In some debates, debaters will diagram on a blackboard the words in the resolution to show how the affirmative is non-topical.

See also: DELIVERY

vocabulary

Definition: The words one can use at any time during a speech.

Example: A debater I saw had an incredible *vocabulary:* she spoke fluently and used many different words.

See also: DELIVERY, LANGUAGE

vocal inflection

Definition: The change in emphasis of one's voice while speaking.

Example: He used *vocal inflection* when he attacked the administration's environmental policies by strongly and sincerely showing concern when he said, "They lack vision." Then he said, "Future generations of children (his voice slightly cracked here, and his voice became more serious) will, (he

emphasized this word even more strongly when he repeated it) WILL get cancer."

See also: MONOTONE, VOCAL VARIETY

vocal quality
Definition: The pleasure that one's vocal tone gives to listeners.
Example: Khoi's whiney voice did not have good *vocal quality.* Gerri's
pleasant tone made her judges agree that she had good *vocal
quality.*
See also: VOCAL TONE

vocal tone
Definition: The sound one's voice makes.
Example: Some people said that George Bush's voice is whiney. Oth-
ers said that Ronald Reagan's voice is soothing and sounds
concerned. These characteristics are these men's *vocal tones.*
See also: MONOTONE, VOCAL QUALITY, VOCAL VARIETY

vocal variety
Definition: The change in one's voice, including speaking at different
rates of speed, changing vocal tone, inflecting, and changing volume.
Example: Jesse Jackson has good *vocal variety* because he changes the
tone of his voice. Darla inflects and varies her voice to make
her message more pleasing.
See also: MONOTONE

voice projection
Definition: The distance one's voice travels; how easy it is to hear a
speaker.
Example: Her poor *voice projection* prevents people at the back of the
room from hearing her speech.
See also: DELIVERY, VOCAL TONE, VOCAL VARIETY

void for vagueness
Definition: To not consider a plan because it is unclear.
Example: Team W argued that the "build some more bombs" plan
was so unclear that it should be declared *void for vagueness.*
See also: CLARIFY, PLAN, VAGUE

voting issue

Definition: A crucial area of argument that must be addressed to support or reject the resolution; an argument that shows the resolution has been supported or rejected.

Example: A disadvantage that shows a plan would greatly increase the risk of war is a *voting issue* since the disadvantage would show that the plan should be rejected.

Usage: This is a clear voting issue for the negative. *(The judge should vote for us on this issue because it shows the resolution should be rejected.)*

See also: ISSUE, STOCK ISSUE

warrant

Definition: The connection between data or evidence and a claim.

Example: If an argument makes the claim "Rollercoasters should be banned," and uses the data "There were 203 people injured or killed on rollercoasters last year," the *warrant* would be "Activities that kill or injure should be banned."

See also: BACKING, CLAIM, DATA, TOULMIN MODEL OF ARGUMENT

Washington style debate

Definition: A debate in which speakers from each side first analyze a problem, then discuss solutions to the problem, and finally, evaluate the desirability of the solutions.

Synonym: PROBLEM SOLVING DEBATE

See also: DEBATE FORMATS

weigh

Definition: To compare the importance of arguments.

Example: The judge *weighed* by comparing the plan's advantages and its disadvantages.

See also: COMPARISON, OUTWEIGH, WEIGHT

weight

Definition: The importance of an argument.

Usage: Since the disadvantage will probably not occur, I gave it little weight in my decision. *(Because the harm to the plan probably will not happen, I didn't consider it important in my decision.)*

See also: ISSUE, PROBABILITY, STOCK ISSUE, VOTING ISSUE, WEIGH

went down

See: GO DOWN

win

Definition: A victory given to the team that the judge feels argued better or presented a stronger case.

Example: Team X *won* the debate when they convinced the judge that Team Y's plan would cause an economic recession.

Usage: Did you win that debate? *(Did the judge vote for you?)*

Antonym: LOSS

See also: DECISION, JUDGE, PARADIGM

word economy

Definition: To state arguments clearly in as few words as possible.

Example: Instead of saying, "The Denver-based car distribution location with that city and its disbursement procedures for giving out cars does indeed work in an effective manner," the debater used *word economy*. She said, "The Denver car distribution center disbursement does work."

See also: CONCISE

workability

Definition: The issue of whether a policy will function effectively.

Example: A plan that pays for home health care may have a *workability* problem because there are so few home health care workers that the plan would not function effectively.

See also: DISADVANTAGE, FIAT, SHOULD-WOULD FALLACY, SOLVENCY

NTC DEBATE AND SPEECH BOOKS

Debate
ADVANCED DEBATE, ed. Thomas & Hart
BASIC DEBATE, Fryar, Thomas, & Goodnight
COACHING AND DIRECTING FORENSICS, Klopf
CROSS-EXAMINATION IN DEBATE, Copeland
DICTIONARY OF DEBATE, Hanson
FORENSIC TOURNAMENTS: PLANNING AND ADMINISTRATION, Goodnight & Zarefsky
GETTING STARTED IN DEBATE, Goodnight
JUDGING ACADEMIC DEBATE, Ulrich
MODERN DEBATE CASE TECHNIQUES, Terry et al.
MOVING FROM POLICY TO VALUE DEBATE, Richards
STRATEGIC DEBATE, Wood & Goodnight
STUDENT CONGRESS & LINCOLN-DOUGLAS DEBATE, Giertz & Mezzera

Speech Communication
ACTIVITIES FOR EFFECTIVE COMMUNICATION, LiSacchi
THE BASICS OF SPEECH, Galvin, Cooper, & Gordon
CONTEMPORARY SPEECH, HopKins & Whitaker
CREATIVE SPEAKING, Buys et al.
DYNAMICS OF SPEECH, Myers & Herndon
GETTING STARTED IN PUBLIC SPEAKING, Prentice & Payne
LISTENING BY DOING, Galvin
LITERATURE ALIVE! Gamble & Gamble
MEETINGS: RULES & PROCEDURES, Pohl
PERSON TO PERSON, Galvin & Book
PUBLIC SPEAKING TODAY! Prentice & Payne
SELF-AWARENESS, Ratliffe & Herman
SPEAKING BY DOING, Buys, Sill, & Beck

For a current catalog and information about our complete line
of language arts books, write:
National Textbook Company,
a division of NTC Publishing Group
4255 West Touhy Avenue
Lincolnwood (Chicago), Illinois 60646-1975 U.S.A.